Grace Abounding

John Bunyan

WORD PUBLISHING
Word (UK) Ltd
Milton Keynes, England
WORD AUSTRALIA
Kilsyth, Victoria, Australia
WORD COMMUNICATIONS LTD
Vancouver, B.C., Canada
STRUIK CHRISTIAN BOOKS (PTY) LTD
Maitland, South Africa
ALBY COMMERCIAL ENTERPRISES PTE LTD
Balmoral Road, Singapore
CHRISTIAN MARKETING NEW ZEALAND LTD
Havelock North, New Zealand
JENSCO LTD
Hong Kong
SALVATION BOOK CENTRE
Malaysia

GRACE ABOUNDING

Published by Word (U.K.) Ltd, 1991

ISBN 0–85009–239–6 (Australia 1–86258–147–9)

Grace Abounding was first published in 1666
The Continuation of Mr Bunyan's life was in 1692
The Relation of his Imprisonment was not published
until 1765

Printed and bound in Great Britain for Word (U.K.) Ltd, by Richard Clay Ltd, Bungay.

91 92 93 94 / 10 9 8 7 6 5 4 3 2 1

CONTENTS

INTRODUCTION

JOHN BUNYAN

1628–1688

JOHN BUNYAN was born at Elstow, near Bedford, in the year 1628. His father was a tinker or brazier. 'For my descent then, it was, as is well known by many, of a low and inconsiderable generation, my father having been of that rank that is meanest and most despised of all the families of the land.' It is, however, only fair to remember that the family of Bunyan had been settled at Elstow for generations, and were apparently held in good repute, and Bunyan's parents were wise enough and able enough to obtain for him the rudiments of education. 'Notwithstanding the meanness and inconsiderableness of my parents, it pleased God to put it into their hearts to put me to school to learn both to read and write, with which I also attained according to the rate of other poor men's children.' Still the surroundings of his childhood were such as would have created incredulity in any one who was told that the name of this boy would become one of the most famous in English literature.

His education at school was brief, and soon of necessity he took part in his father's trade. He had in early youth the sorrow to lose his mother and a sister. But whatever impression the sorrow made upon him, it was transient, and he led a thoughtless life. The language in which he speaks of himself appears exaggerated to those who are ignorant of the reality of spiritual conflict. They have considered the portrait which he has painted of himself as utterly blackened and distorted. They have seen nothing in his career to warrant his use of such self-reproachful terms, and have been inclined to treat the whole story of those dark days as a hallucination. What about robbing orchards, or swearing? they ask. These things were done by the young men of that time, and especially by those of Bunyan's rank, without compunction, without any thought of harm; and that he should so grieve over such words and deeds arose mainly from unusual morbidity. Bunyan looked beneath the surface. Compared with others, his life may have been blameless; but he did not compare it with that of others. A higher ideal had come before his soul. He looked at his life in the light of the Law of God, and the vision filled him with dismay; he saw himself so imperfect, so sinful. Testing his conduct, not by conventional standards, but by the standard of the All Holy, he felt himself in very truth the chief of sinners. His misery was increased by his attempts to be contented with the ordinary life of those around him. He tried to be deaf to the Voice which was calling him to higher things. He would fain enjoy the amusements which his companions enjoyed, but every now and again, by tormenting thoughts and terrifying dreams, he was a burden to himself.

In 1645 he served for a short time as a soldier. It has been doubted whether he was in the Royalist or the Parliamentary army; and it is very singular that from his own writings it is impossible to solve the question. He was so absorbed in the spiritual phases through which he had passed, he was so persuaded of their infinite importance, that mere outward incidents seemed hardly worth the mentioning. Lord Macaulay took it for granted that he fought in the Parliamentary ranks. Mr. Froude thinks it more likely that, as it was a matter of levying, not of volunteering, he fought in the ranks of the Royalists. Weighing the evidence carefully, Dr. Brown of Bedford comes to the conclusion that Lord Macaulay was right, and that, in obedience to the behest of the Parliament, he gained the experience of military life which enabled him to give additional accuracy and vividness to various scenes and characters in *The Pilgrim's Progress* and *The Holy War*. On whichever side he was, a narrow escape which he made filled him afterwards with mingled shuddering and thanksgiving. 'When I was a soldier, I, with others, was drawn out to go to such a place to besiege it; but when I was just ready to go, one of the company desired to go in my room; to which when I had consented, he took my place, and coming to the siege, as he stood sentinel, he was shot into the head with a musket bullet, and died.'

He was married in the year 1649 when scarcely twenty-one. The name of his wife is altogether unknown, but her influence upon him was for good. 'My mercy was to light upon a wife whose father was counted godly. This woman and I, though we came together as poor as poor might be, not having so much household stuff as a dish or spoon betwixt us both, yet this she had for her part, *The Plain Man's Pathway to Heaven*, and *The Practice of Piety*, which her father had left her when he died.' Bunyan now became very regular in his attendance at Church, and was seized with a superstitious reverence for sacred things. 'I adored, and that with great devotion, even all things, both the high place, priest, clerk, vestment, service, and what else belonging to the Church, counting all things holy that were therein contained, and especially the priest and clerk most happy, and without doubt greatly blessed, because they were the servants, as I then thought, of God, and were principal in the holy temple to do His work therein.'

He was once more plunged into great despondency. He looked in every direction for relief, but could find none. He thought if he could prove himself to be of Israelitish origin it would be well with him. He fancied that he had committed the unpardonable sin, and a very foolish, though aged, person from whom he sought consolation, gravely answered, 'I think you have.' 'Here, therefore, I had but cold comfort; but talking a little more with him, I found him, though a good man, a stranger to much combat with the devil. Wherefore I went to God again, as well as I could, for mercy still.' Bunyan was to continue to be no stranger to combat. He had to fight against all manner of temptations to unbelief and blasphemy. Yet all the while he trembled at the thought of death and judgment; and bell-ringing and other innocent recreations, though persisted in, were regarded as sins.

Stimulated by overhearing some poor women speak of the joy which they had in their faith, he aspired to have the same, and thought to prove his faith by working miracles. Glimpses of peace were granted to him at times. 'One day,' for example, 'after I had been so many weeks oppressed and cast down therewith, as I was now quite giving up the ghost of all my hopes of ever attaining life, that sentence fell with weight upon my spirit: "Look at the generations of old and see; did ever any trust in the Lord, and was confounded?" ' For that verse he searched the Bible from Genesis to Revelation in vain; and it was not till after the lapse of a year that he accidentally discovered it in the Apocryphal Book of Ecclesiasticus. 'This,' he says with touching simplicity, 'at first did somewhat daunt me, but because by this time I had got more experience of the love and kindness of God, it troubled me the less; especially when I considered that though it was not in those texts which are called holy and canonical, yet forasmuch as this sentence was the sum and substance of the promises, it was my duty to take the comfort of it; and I bless God for that word, for it was of God to me; that word doth still, at times, shine before my face.'

So, after 'many a sorrow, many a labour, many a tear,' he arrived at settled convictions, and the peace which passeth understanding. There was a congregation at Bedford to which he was led to attach himself. In this congregation baptism was an open question. The minister was John Gifford, who had at one time been a major in the Royalist army. He had been a reckless, irreligious man, but he led, after his conversion, a steady, consistent life to the end. Amid the curious confusions of the time, when the ecclesiastical conditions of the country were for a few years different from what they ever were before or have ever been since, Gifford, Congregationalist and Baptist though he was, received from the Corporation the presentation of the living, which had become vacant by the death of the rector. Gifford was a man of vigour, and even at the present day a letter, which Southey describes as 'wise, tolerant, and truly Christian,' is annually read in the congregation which he founded. This letter was written on his death-bed, and contained his parting instructions. He counsels his flock to keep together after he is gone, for they are not 'joined to the ministry, but to Christ and the Church.' He warns them against divisions. 'Concerning separation from the Church about baptism, laying on of hands, anointing with oil, psalms, or any externals, I charge every one of you respectively, as you will give an account of it to our Lord Jesus Christ, who shall judge both quick and dead at His coming, that none of you be found guilty of this great evil.' And commending the congregation to God, and signing the letter with his own hand, John Gifford departed.

In the congregation of this remarkable man Bunyan occupied a prominent place. He was a deacon, and was, after a time, asked to preach in various places. It was with unfeigned reluctance that he consented to address meetings. His powers were, however, so marked that he was soon in such request as a preacher that he had to relinquish his duties as deacon. The intense earnestness and reality of his words made a profound impression wherever he went. 'I went myself in chains to preach to them in chains, and carried that fire in my own conscience that I persuaded them to beware of.'

Nor was it only by speaking but by writing that he sought to win men to Christ. His first book was published in the year 1956, and was entitled *Some Gospel Truths Opened*. It was of a controversial nature, and was directed against the Quakers. Edward Burroughs, a Quaker of note and ability, defended their doctrine, and the contest between these excellent men grew very hot. But although Bunyan was so zealous against one set of Nonconformists, his own opinions and actions were equally unpalatable to the ecclesiastical authorities after the Restoration. He was attacked by clergymen for his assumption of the teaching office, and was constantly jeered at as a tinker.

At length, as he did not attend the parish church, and as meetings for worship such as he conducted were

declared illegal, he was, at the instance of Mr. Francis
Wingate, a neighbouring magistrate, arrested as he was
about to address a company of people assembled in a
private house at Lower Samsell. He has told, with
considerable detail, the story of his interview with his
judges. The law was an unrighteous law, and some of
those before whom he was brought were prejudiced and
unreasonable. Still it is just to observe that, on the
whole, there was an evident desire to deal leniently with
him. As, however, he could not in conscience accede to
what they in law were bound to demand, his trial could
have only one termination, and he was sentenced to
imprisonment. To a man of his active temperament and
affectionate disposition, it was a terrible hardship. 'The
parting with my wife and poor children hath oft been to
me in this place as the pulling the flesh from my bones,
and that not only because I am somewhat too fond of
these great mercies, but also because I should have often
brought to my mind the many hardships, miseries, and
wants that my poor family was like to meet with should I
be taken from them; especially my poor blind child, who
lay nearer my heart than all I had besides. Poor child,
thought I, what sorrow art thou like to have for thy
portion in this world? Thou must be beaten, must
beg, suffer hunger, cold, nakedness, and a thousand
calamities, though I cannot now endure the wind to blow
upon thee. . . . O, I said, in this condition I was as a man
who was pulling down his house upon the head of his
wife and children; yet, thought I, I must do it, I must do
it.'

His second wife, a noble woman, made many efforts to
obtain his release, but in vain. When Charles II was
crowned, an act of forgiveness was proclaimed to
multitudes of prisoners, but Bunyan was not allowed to
escape. Barabbas was set at liberty, but the humble
disciple of Christ had to remain. His imprisonment
lasted about twelve years. He appears to have had a
certain amount of liberty; he saw friends from time to
time; he was occasionally allowed to leave the prison
walls; he made a living by making and selling long-

tagged laces; and he spent much time in writing. It was not, however, during these twelve years that he wrote *The Pilgrim's Progress*. The works which were the outcome of this imprisonment were: *Profitable Meditations, Praying in Spirit, Christian Behaviour*, and *Grace Abounding*. His library in prison consisted almost solely of two books—the Bible and Foxe's *Book of Martyrs*.

On the 8th of May 1672, when he was forty-four years of age, Bunyan was set free. This was in consequence of a Declaration of Indulgence intended by the King to benefit Roman Catholics, but as they could hardly be tolerated without tolerating others who did not belong to the Church of England, all Nonconformists were included in the Declaration. It is no matter for surprise that the congregation of which he had been a member, and which had for some years been without a pastor, insisted on his accepting the office. And so far did his influence extend, so frequently did he preach elsewhere, that he was popularly called Bishop Bunyan.

After three years of liberty he was once more in prison, in consequence of another Test Act which was aimed especially at Roman Catholics, but in its working included all Nonconformists from the Church of England. Previously he had been in the county gaol at Bedford. This time he was in the small and miserable town gaol on Bedford Bridge; and it was during this imprisonment, which lasted only six months, that he began *The Pilgrim's Progress*. Internal evidence seems to prove that in prison he wrote as far as the parting of Christian and Hopeful with the Shepherds on the Delectable Mountains, and that he completed Part I after his release. This first edition did not contain some passages which are now among the most memorable in the volume, *e.g.* there is nothing about Mr. Worldly Wiseman; Christian's discourse with Charity at the Palace Beautiful; Mr. Byends; Diffidence, the wife of Giant Despair; or the pilgrims being met on the farther side of the river by the King's trumpeters in white and shining raiment. Bunyan's final release was obtained by the intervention of Dr. Barlow, Bishop of Lincoln. The rest of his days were spent in comparative peace. He was never weary in his labours to extend the kingdom of God. He wrote *The Life and Death of Mr. Badman*, as a kind of companion and contrast to the Pilgrimage of Christian. He wrote *The Holy War*, the Second Part of *The Pilgrim's Progress*, and a number of works of less importance, though some of them, such as *The Jerusalem Sinner Saved*, contain passages of great power and beauty. His reputation always increased. 'When Mr. Bunyan preached in London,' says a contemporary, 'if there were but one day's notice given, there would be more people come together to hear him preach than the meeting-house could hold. I have seen to hear him preach, by my computation, about twelve hundred at a morning lecture by seven o'clock on a working-day, in the dark winter-time. I also computed about three thousand that came to hear him one Lord's Day at London, at a town's end meeting-house, so that half were fain to go back again for want of room, and then himself was fain at a back door to be pulled almost over people to get upstairs to his pulpit.'

Bunyan's death was worthy of his life. He caught his fatal illness in a work of reconciliation. He went round by Reading, on his way to London, in August 1688, in order to make peace between a father and son who had become estranged. This mission accomplished, he set off for London, and rode the forty miles through drenching rain. He was still able to preach once or twice, and to see his publisher about a treatise on the Fifty-first Psalm, but he never recovered from the chill with which he had been struck on that dreary ride. On the 31st August 1688, at the house of John Stradwick, Grocer, Snowhill, his earthly pilgrimage was ended.

What has given the writings of Bunyan their peculiar charm? He wrote with great directness and simplicity. Nobody can ever be at a loss to understand what he means. The common people have always heard him gladly; but as it is human nature which he unveils, there is no class, educated or uneducated, to which he does not appeal.

He wrote out of a full heart. His works are the simple

expression of his honest, unaffected nature. He simply describes what he has seen and known. The profoundest passages, which betray such a marvellous acquaintance with the intricacies of the spiritual life, and which have hardly any parallel, unless it be the seventh chapter of the Epistle to the Romans, are merely the record of his own experience. His dramatic power is almost un-surpassed. The picture gallery which he has provided for the benefit of the world contains innumerable portraits, and they are in the most natural manner distinguishable from each other.

He was, with whatever limitations of Puritanism, of a large and Catholic heart. All sections of Christendom have been able to use his greatest allegory, and have found in it the statement of their own deepest needs and faith. 'You ask me,' he once wrote, 'how long is it since I was a Baptist? I must tell you I know none to whom that title is so proper as to the disciples of John. And since you would know by what name I would be distinguished from others, I tell you I would be, and hope I am, a Christian, and choose, if God should count me worthy, to be called a Christian, a believer, or other such name as is approved by the Holy Ghost. And as for those titles of Anabaptists, Independents, Presbyterians, or the like, I conclude that they come neither from Jerusalem nor Antioch, but rather from hell and Babylon, for they naturally tend to division. You may know them by their fruits.' He was at one time most severe in his censure of all who would use a book of Common Prayer; in later days he had come to acknowledge that the abandoment of a form of prayer was no security for the attainment of its spirit.

He had great dread of that style of teaching which tells people they have nothing to do but believe; that once they turn to God all is plain afterwards. With what truth, with what exquisite sympathy, is this theory refuted in *The Pilgrim's Progress*. What conflicts, what sorrows, what temptations, await Christian after he has left the City of Destruction, after he has met Evangelist, after he has been through the Valley of the Shadow of Death. What a variety of characters, who, destitute of assurance, are yet genuine believers, and who yet have to plod wearily on in depression: Mr. Fearing, Feeble-Mind, Ready to Halt. With what humour and sarcasm has he shown the necessity of reality, in the characters, for example, of the hypocritical Byends, and of the chattering, superficial Talkative. 'Religion hath no place in his heart or house or conversation; all he hath lieth in his tongue, and his religion is to make a noise therewith.'

Bunyan was not a learned theologian or apologist. He may not help the perplexed amid critical or scientific difficulties. He belonged to the seventeenth century, not to the twentieth. But still and for ever more, his books will appeal to the minds of men; for, with whatever traces of the dialect of his own day and his own school, he is occupied with truths which are universal and eternal; he is commending not so much any special aspect of opinion as Him who is the great object of all Christian teaching, Him who is the same yesterday, and to-day, and for ever. The Holy War, of which Bunyan has written, is a war from which none of us can obtain a discharge. The Grace Abounding, which he gratefully extolled, is the grace to which we have all to trust.

A PREFACE, OR BRIEF ACCOUNT
OF THE PUBLISHING OF
THIS WORK

WRITTEN BY THE AUTHOR THEREOF, AND DEDICATED TO
THOSE WHOM GOD HATH COUNTED HIM WORTHY TO
BEGET TO FAITH, BY HIS MINISTRY IN THE WORD

CHILDREN, grace be with you, Amen. I being taken from you in presence, and so tied up, that I cannot perform that duty that from God doth lie upon me to youward, for your further edifying and building up in faith and holiness, etc., yet that you may see my soul hath fatherly care and desire after your spiritual and everlasting welfare; I now once again, as before, from the top of Shenir and Hermon, so now from the lions' dens, from the mountains of the leopards (Song iv. 8), do look yet after you all, greatly longing to see your safe arrival into the desired haven.

I thank God upon every remembrance of you; and rejoice, even while I stick between the teeth of the lions in the wilderness, at the grace, and mercy, and knowledge of Christ our Saviour, which God hath bestowed upon you, with abundance of faith and love. Your hungerings and thirstings also after further acquaintance with the Father, in his Son; your tenderness of heart, your trembling at sin, your sober and holy deportment also, before both God and men, is great refreshment to me; "For ye are my glory and joy" (*1 Thess. ii.* 20).

I have sent you here enclosed, a drop of that honey, that I have taken out of the carcase of a lion (*Judges xiv.* 5–9). I have eaten thereof myself also, and am much refreshed thereby. (Temptations, when we meet them at first, are as the lion that roared upon Samson; but if we overcome them, the next time we see them, we shall find a nest of honey within them.) The Philistines understand me not. It is something of a relation of the work of

God upon my own soul, even from the very first, till now; wherein you may perceive my castings down, and raisings up; for he woundeth, and his hands make whole. It is written in the Scripture (*Is. xxxviii. 19*), "The father to the children shall make known the truth of God." Yea, it was for this reason I lay so long at Sinai (*Deut. iv. 10, 11*), to see the fire, and the cloud, and the darkness, that I might fear the Lord all the days of my life upon earth, and tell of his wondrous works to my children (*Ps. lxxviii. 3–5*).

Moses (*Num. xxxiii. 1, 2*) writ of the journeyings of the children of Israel, from Egypt to the land of Canaan; and commanded also, that they did remember their forty years' travel in the wilderness. "Thou shalt remember all the way which the Lord thy God led thee these forty years in the wilderness, to humble thee, *and* to prove thee, to know what *was* in thine heart, whether thou wouldest keep his commandments, or no" (*Deut. viii. 2*). Wherefore this I have endeavoured to do; and not only so, but to publish it also; that, if God will, others may be put in remembrance of what he hath done for their souls, by reading his work upon me.

It is profitable for Christians to be often calling to mind the very beginnings of grace with their souls. "It *is* a night to be much observed unto the Lord for bringing them out from the land of Egypt: this *is* that night of the Lord to be observed of all the children of Israel in their generations" (*Exod. xii. 42*). "O my god," saith David (*Ps. xlii. 6*), "MY SOUL IS CAST DOWN WITHIN ME; THERE-FORE WILL I REMEMBER THEE FROM THE LAND OF JORDAN, AND OF THE HERMONITES, FROM THE HILL MIZAR." HE REMEMBERED ALSO THE LION AND THE BEAR, WHEN HE WENT TO fIGHT WITH THE GIANT OF GATH (*1 Sam. xvii. 36, 37*).

It was Paul's accustomed manner (*Acts xxii*), and that when tried for his life (*Acts xxiv*), ever to open, before his judges, the manner of his conversion: he would think of that day, and that hour, in the which he first did meet with grace; for he found it support unto him. When God had brought the children of Israel through the Red Sea, far into the wilderness, yet they must turn quite about thither again, to remember the drowning of their enemies there (*Num. xiv. 25*). For though they sang his praise before, yet "they soon forgat his works" (*Ps. cvi. 11–13*).

In this discourse of mine you may see much; much, I say, of the grace of God towards me. I thank God I can count it much, for it was above my sins and Satan's temptations too. I can remember my fears, and doubts, and sad months with comfort; they are as the head of Goliath in my hand. There was nothing to David like Goliath's sword, even that sword that should have been sheathed in his bowels; for the very sight and remembrance of that did preach forth God's deliverance to him. Oh, the remembrance of my great sins, of my great temptations, and of my great fears of perishing for ever! They bring afresh into my mind the remembrance of my great help, my great support from heaven, and the great grace that God extended to such a wretch as I.

My dear children, call to mind the former days, "and the years of ancient times: remember also your songs in the night; and commune with your own heart" (*Ps. lxxvii. 5–12*). Yea, look diligently, and leave no corner therein unsearched, for there is treasure hid, even the treasure of your first and second experience of the grace of God toward you. Remember, I say, the word that first laid hold upon you; remember also your terrors of conscience, and fear of death, and hell; tears and prayers to God; yea, how you sighed under every hedge for mercy. Have you never a hill Mizar to remember? Have you forgot the close, the milk house, the stable, the barn, and the like, where God did visit your soul? Remember also the Word—the Word, I say, upon which the Lord hath caused you to hope. If you have sinned against light; if you are tempted to blaspheme; if you are down in despair; if you think God fights against you; or if heaven is hid from your eyes, remember it was thus with your father, but out of them all the Lord delivered me.

I could have enlarged much in this my discourse, of my temptations and troubles for sin; as also of the merciful kindness and working of God with my soul. I could also have stepped into a style much higher than this in which I have here discoursed, and could have adorned all things more than here I have seemed to do, but I dare not. God did not play in convincing of me, the devil did not play in tempting of me, neither did I play when I sunk as into a bottomless pit, when the pangs of hell caught hold upon me; wherefore I may not play in my relating of them, but be plain and simple, and lay down the thing as it was. He that liketh it, let him receive it; and he that does not, let him produce a better. Farewell.

My dear children, the milk and honey is beyond this wilderness. God be merciful to you, and grant that you be not slothful to go in to posssess the land.

JOHN BUNYAN.

GRACE ABOUNDING TO THE CHIEF OF SINNERS

OR, A BRIEF RELATION OF THE EXCEEDING MERCY
OR GOD IN CHRIST, TO HIS POOR SERVANT JOHN
BUNYAN

1. In this my relation of the merciful working of God upon my soul, it will not be amiss, if, in the first place, I do, in a few words, give you a hint of my pedigree, and manner of bringing up; that thereby the goodness and bounty of God towards me, may be the more advanced and magnified before the sons of men.

2. For my descent then, it was, as is well known by many, of a low and inconsiderable generation; my father's house being of that rank that is meanest and most despised of all the families in the land. Wherefore I have not here, as others, to boast of noble blood, or of a high-born state, according to the flesh; though, all things considered, I magnify the heavenly Majesty, for that by this door he brought me into this world, to partake of the grace and life that is in Christ by the gospel.

3. But yet, notwithstanding the meanness and inconsiderableness of my parents, it pleased God to put it into their hearts to put me to school, to learn both to read and write; the which I also attained, according to the rate of other poor men's children; though, to may shame I confess, I did soon lose that little I learned and that even almost utterly, and that long before the Lord did work his gracious work of conversion upon my soul.

4. As for my own natural life, for the time that I was without God in the world, it was indeed according to the course of this world, and "the spirit that now worketh in the children of disobedience" (*Eph. ii. 2, 3*). It was my delight to be "taken captive by the devil at his will" (*2 Tim. ii. 26*). Being filled with all unrighteousness: the

which did also so strongly work and put forth itself, both in my heart and life, and that from a child, that I had but few equals, especially considering my years, which were tender, being few, both for cursing, swearing, lying, and blaspheming the holy name of God.

5. Yea, so settled and rooted was I in these things, that they became as a second nature to me; the which, as I also have with soberness considered since, did so offend the Lord, that even in my childhood he did scare and affright me with fearful dreams, and did terrify me with dreadful visions; for often, after I had spent this and the other day in sin, I have in my bed been greatly afflicted, while asleep, with the apprehensions of devils and wicked spirits, who still, as I then thought, laboured to draw me away with them, of which I could never be rid.

6. Also I should, at these years, be greatly afflicted and troubled with the thoughts of the day of judgment, and that both night and day, and should tremble at the thoughts of the fearful torments of hell fire; still fearing that it would be my lot to be found at last amongst those devils and hellish fiends, who are there bound down with the chains and bonds of eternal darkness, "unto the judgment of the great day."

7. These things, I say, when I was but a child but nine or ten years old, did so distress my soul, that when in the midst of my many sports and childish vanities, amidst my vain companions, I was often much cast down and afflicted in my mind therewith, yet could I not let go my sins. Yea, I was also then so overcome with despair of life and heaven, that I should often wish either that there had been no hell, or that I had been a devil—supposing they were only tormentors; that if it must needs be that I went thither, I might be rather a tormentor, than be tormented myself.

8. A while after, these terrible dreams did leave me, which also I soon forgot; for my pleasures did quickly cut off the remembrance of them, as if they had never been: wherefore, with more greediness, according to the strength of nature, I did still let loose the reins to my lusts, and delighted in all transgression against the law of

God: so that, until I came to the state of marriage, I was the very ringleader of all the youth that kept me company, into all manner of vice and ungodliness.

9. Yea, such prevalency had the lusts and fruits of the flesh in this poor soul of mine, that had not a miracle of precious grace prevented, I had not only perished by the stroke of eternal justice, but had also laid myself open, even to the stroke of those laws, which bring some to disgrace and open shame before the face of the world.

10. In these days, the thoughts of religion were very grievous to me; I could neither endure it myself, nor that any other should; so that, when I have seen some read in those books that concerned Christian piety, it would be as it were a prison to me. Then I said unto God, "Depart from me, for I desire not the knowledge of thy ways" (*Job xxi. 14*). I was now void of all good consideration, heaven and hell were both out of sight and mind; and as for saving and damning, they were least in my thoughts. O Lord, thou knowest my life, and my ways were not hid from thee.

11. Yet this I well remember, that though I could myself sin with the greatest delight and ease, and also take pleasure in the vileness of my companions; yet, even then, if I have at any time seen wicked things, by those who professed goodness, it would make my spirit tremble. As once, above all the rest, when I was in my height of vanity, yet hearing one to swear that was reckoned for a religious man, it had so great a stroke upon my spirit, that it made my heart to ache.

12. But God did not utterly leave me, but followed me still, not now wich convictions, but judgments; yet such as were mixed with mercy. For once I fell into a creek of the sea, and hardly escaped drowning. Another time I fell out of a boat into Bedford river, but mercy yet preserved me alive. Besides, another time, being in the field with one of my companions, it chanced that an adder passed over the highway; so I, having a stick in my hand, struck her over the back; and having stunned her, I forced open her mouth with my stick, and plucked her sting out with my fingers; by which act, had not God

been merciful unto me, I might, by my desperateness, have brought myself to mine end.

13. This also have I taken notice of with thanksgiving; when I was a soldier, I, with others, were drawn out to go to such a place to besiege it; but when I was just ready to go, one of the company desired to go in my room; to which, when I had consented, he took my place; and coming to the siege, as he stood sentinel, he was shot into the head with a musket bullet, and died.

14. Here, as I said, were judgments and mercy, but neither of them did awaken my soul to righteousness; wherefore I sinned still, and grew more and more rebellious against God, and careless of mine own salvation.

15. Presently after this, I changed my condition into a married state, and my mercy was to light upon a wife whose father was counted godly. This woman and I, though we came together as poor as poor might be, not having so much household stuff as a dish or spoon betwixt us both, yet this she had for her part, *The Plain Man's Pathway to Heaven*, and *The Practice of Piety*, which her father had left her when he died. In these two books I should sometimes read with her, wherein I also found some things that were somewhat pleasing to me; but all this while I met with no conviction. She also would be often telling of me, what a godly man her father was, and how he would reprove and correct vice, both in his house, and amongst his neighbours; what a strict and holy life he lived in his day, both in word and deed.

16. Wherefore these books with this relation, though they did not reach my heart, to awaken it about my sad and sinful state, yet they did beget within me some desires to religion: so that, because I knew no better, I fell in very eagerly with the religion of the times; to wit, to go to church twice a day, and that too with the foremost; and there should very devoutly, both say and sing as others did, yet retaining my wicked life; but withal, I was so overrun with a spirit of superstition, that I adored, and that with great devotion, even all things, both the high place, priest, clerk, vestment, service, and

what else belonging to the church; counting all things holy that were therein contained, and especially the priest and clerk most happy, and without doubt, greatly blessed, because they were the servants, as I then thought, of God, and were principal in the holy temple, to do his work therein.

17. This conceit grew so strong in little time upon my spirit, that had I but seen a priest, though never so sordid and debauched in his life, I should find my spirit fall under him, reverence him, and knit unto him; yea, I thought for the love I did bear unto them, supposing they were the ministers of God, I could have lain down at their feet, and have been trampled upon by them; their name, their garb, and work, did so intoxicate and bewitch me.

18. After I had been thus for some considerable time, another thought came into my mind; and that was, whether we were of the Israelites, or no? For finding in the Scriptures that they were once the peculiar people of God, thought I, if I were one of this race, my soul must needs be happy. Now again, I found within me a great longing to be resolved about this question, but could not tell how I should. At last I asked my father of it; who told me, No, we were not. Wherefore then I fell in my spirit as to the hopes of that, and so remained.

19. But all this while, I was not sensible of the danger and evil of sin; I was kept from considering that sin would damn me, what religion soever I followed, unless I was found in Christ. Nay, I never thought of him, nor whether there was one, or no. Thus man, while blind, doth wander, but wearieth himself with vanity, for he knoweth not the way to the city of God (*Eccles. x. 15*).

20. But one day, amongst all the sermons our parson made, his subject was, to treat of the Sabbath-day, and of the evil of breaking that, either with labour, sports, or otherwise. Now I was, notwithstanding my religion, one that took much delight in all manner of vice, and especially that was the day that I did solace myself therewith, wherefore I fell in my conscience under his sermon, thinking and believing that he made that

sermon on purpose to show me my evil doing; and at that time I felt what guilt was, though never before, that I can remember; but then I was, for the present, greatly loaden therewith, and so went home when the sermon was ended, with a great burden upon my spirit.

21. This, for that instant, did benumb the sinews of my best delights, and did imbitter my former pleasures to me; but behold, it lasted not, for before I had well dined, the trouble began to go off my mind, and my heart returned to its old course: but oh! how glad was I, that this trouble was gone from me, and that the fire was put out, that I might sin again without control! Wherefore, when I had satisfied nature with my food, I shook the sermon out of my mind, and to my old custom of sports and gaming I returned with great delight.

22. But the same day, as I was in the midst of a game at cat, and having struck it one blow from the hole, just as I was about to strike it the second time, a voice did suddenly dart from heaven into my soul, which said, Wilt thou leave thy sins and go to heaven, or have thy sins and go to hell? At this I was put to an exceeding maze; wherefore, leaving my cat upon the ground, I looked up to heaven, and was, as if I had, with the eyes of my understanding, seen the Lord Jesus looking down upon me, as being very hotly displeased with me, and as if he did severely threaten me with some grievous punishment for these and other my ungodly practices.

23. I had no sooner thus conceived in my mind, but suddenly this conclusion was fastened on my spirit, for the former hint did set my sins again before my face, that I had been a great and grievous sinner, and that it was now too late for me to look after heaven; for Christ would not forgive me, nor pardon my transgressions. Then I fell to musing upon this also; and while I was thinking on it, and fearing lest it should be so, I felt my heart sink in despair, concluding it was too late; and therefore I resolved in my mind I would go on in sin: for, thought I, if the case be thus, my state is surely miserable; miserable if I leave my sins, and but miserable if I follow them; I can but be damned, and if I must be so, I had as

good be damned for many sins, as to be damned for few.

24. Thus I stood in the midst of my play, before all that then were present; but yet I told them nothing: but I say, I having made this conclusion, I returned desperately to my sport again; and I well remember, that presently this kind of despair did so possess my soul, that I was persuaded I could never attain to other comfort than what I should get in sin; for heaven was gone already, so that on that I must not think; wherefore I found within me a great desire to take my fill of sin, still studying what sin was yet to be committed, that I might taste the sweetness of it; and I made as much haste as I could to fill my belly with its delicates, lest I should die before I had my desire; for that I feared greatly. In these things, I protest before God, I lie not, neither do I feign this sort of speech; these were really, strongly, and with all my heart, my desires; the good Lord, whose mercy is unsearchable, forgive me my transgressions.

25. And I am very confident, that this temptation of the devil is more usual amongst poor creatures than many are aware of, even to overrun their spirits with a scurvy and seared frame of heart, and benumbing of conscience; which frame, he stilly and slily supplieth with such despair, that though not much guilt attendeth the soul, yet they continually have a secret conclusion within them, that there is no hopes for them; for they have loved sins, "therefore after them they will go" (*Jer. ii. 25; xviii. 12*).

26. Now therefore I went on in sin with great greediness of mind, still grudging that I could not be so satisfied with it as I would. This did continue with me about a month, or more; but one day, as I was standing at a neighbour's shopwindow, and there cursing and swearing, and playing the madman, after my wonted manner, there sat within the woman of the house, and heard me, who, though she was a very loose and ungodly wretch, yet protested that I swore and cursed at that most fearful rate, that she was made to tremble to hear me; and told me further, That I was the ungodliest fellow for swearing that ever she heard in all her life; and that I,

by thus doing, was able to spoil all the youth in a whole town, if they came but in my company.

27. At this reproof I was silenced, and put to secret shame, and that too, as I thought, before the God of heaven; wherefore, while I stood there, and hanging down my head, I wished with all my heart that I might be a little child again, that my father might learn me to speak without this wicked way of swearing; for, thought I, I am so accustomed to it, that it is in vain for me to think of a reformation, for I thought it could never be.

28. But how it came to pass, I know not; I did from this time forward so leave my swearing, that it was a great wonder to myself to observe it; and whereas before, I knew not how to speak unless I put an oath before, and another behind, to make my words have authority; now, I could, without it, speak better, and with more pleasantness, than ever I could before. All this while I knew not Jesus Christ, neither did I leave my sports and plays.

29. But quickly after this, I fell in company with one poor man that made profession of religion; who, as I then thought, did talk pleasantly of the Scriptures, and of the matters of religion; wherefore, falling into some love and liking to what he said, I betook me to my Bible, and began to take great pleasure in reading, but especially with the historical part thereof; for, as for Paul's epistles, and Scriptures of that nature, I could not away with them, being as yet but ignorant, either of the corruptions of my nature, or of the want and worth of Jesus Christ to save me.

30. Wherefore I fell to some outward reformation, both in my words and life, and did set the commandments before me for my way to heaven; which commandments I also did strive to keep, and, as I thought, did keep them pretty well sometimes, and then I should have comfort; yet now and then should break one, and so afflict my conscience; but then I should repent, and say I was sorry for it, and promise God to do better next time, and there get help again, for then I thought I pleased God as well as any man in England.

31. Thus I continued about a year; all which time our

neighbours did take me to be a very godly man, a new and religious man, and did marvel much to see such a great and famous alteration in my life and manners; and, indeed, so it was, though yet I knew not Christ, nor grace, nor faith, nor hope; and, truly, as I have well seen since, had I then died, my state had been most fearful; well, this, I say, continued about a twelvemonth or more.

32. But, I say, my neighbours were amazed at this my great conversion, from prodigious profaneness, to something like a moral life; and, truly, so they well might; for this my conversion was as great, as for Tom of Bedlam to become a sober man. Now, therefore, they began to praise, to commend, and to speak well of me, both to my face, and behind my back. Now, I was, as they said, become godly; now, I was become a right honest man. But, Oh! when I understood that these were their words and opinions of me, it pleased me mighty well. For though, as yet, I was nothing but a poor painted hypocrite, yet I loved to be talked of as one that was truly godly. I was proud of my godliness, and, indeed, I did all I did, either to be seen of, or to be well spoken of, by man. And thus I continued for about a twelvemonth or more.

33. Now, you must know, that before this I had taken much delight in ringing, but my conscience beginning to be tender, I thought such practice was but vain, and therefore forced myself to leave it, yet my mind hankered; wherefore I should go to the steeple house, and look on it, though I durst not ring. But I thought this did not become religion neither, yet I forced myself, and would look on still; but quickly after, I began to think, How, if one of the bells should fall? Then I chose to stand under a main beam, that lay overthwart the steeple, from side to side, thinking there I might stand sure, but then I should think again, should the bell fall with a swing, it might first hit the wall, and then rebounding upon me, might kill me for all this beam. This made me stand in the steeple door; and now, thought I, I am safe enough; for, if a bell should then fall, I can slip out behind these thick walls, and so be preserved notwithstanding.

34. So, after this, I would yet go to see them ring, but would not go farther than the steeple door; but then it came into my head, How, if the steeple itself should fall? And this thought, it may fall for aught I know, when I stood and looked on, did continually so shake my mind, that I durst not stand at the steeple door any longer, but was forced to flee, for fear the steeple should fall upon my head.

35. Another thing was my dancing; I was a full year before I could quite leave that; but all this while, when I thought I kept this or that commandment, or did, by word or deed, anything that I thought was good, I had great peace in my conscience; and should think with myself, God cannot choose but be now pleased with me; yea, to relate it in mine own way, I thought no man in England could please God better than I.

36. But poor wretch as I was, I was all this while ignorant of Jesus Christ, and going about to establish my own righteousness; and had perished therein, had not God, in mercy, showed me more of my state of nature.

37. But upon a day, the good providence of God did cast me to Bedford, to work on my calling; and in one of the streets of that town, I came where there were three or four poor women sitting at a door in the sun, and talking about the things of God; and being now willing to hear them discourse, I drew near to hear what they said, for I was now a brisk talker also myself in the matters of religion, but now I may say, I heard, but I understood not; for they were far above, out of my reach; for their talk was about a new birth, the work of God on their hearts, also how they were convinced of their miserable state by nature; they talked how God had visited their souls with his love in the Lord Jesus, and with what words and promises they had been refreshed, comforted, and supported against the temptations of the devil. Moreover, they reasoned of the suggestions and temptations of Satan in particular; and told to each other by which they had been afflicted, and how they were borne up under his assaults. They also discoursed of their own wretchedness of heart, of their unbelief; and did

contemn, slight, and abhor their own righteousness, as filthy and insufficient to do them any good.

38. And methought they spake as if joy did make them speak; they spake with such pleasantness of Scripture language, and with such appearance of grace in all they said, that they were to me as if they had found a new world, as if they were people that dwelt alone, and were not to be reckoned among their neighbours (*Num. xxiii. 9*).

39. At this I felt my own heart began to shake, as mistrusting my condition to be naught; for I saw that in all my thoughts about religion and salvation, the new birth did never enter into my mind, neither knew I the comfort of the Word and promise, nor the deceitfulness and treachery of my own wicked heart. As for secret thoughts, I took no notice of them; neither did I understand what Satan's temptations were, nor how they were to be withstood and resisted, etc.

40. Thus, therefore, when I had heard and considered what they said, I left them, and went about my employment again, but their talk and discourse went with me; also my heart would tarry with them, for I was greatly affected with their words, both because by them I was convinced that I wanted the true tokens of a truly godly man, and also because by them I was convinced of the happy and blessed condition of him that was such a one.

41. Therefore I should often make it my business to be going again and again into the company of these poor people, for I could not stay away; and the more I went amongst them, the more I did question my condition; and as I still do remember, presently I found two things within me, at which I did sometimes marvel, especially considering what a blind, ignorant, sordid, and ungodly wretch but just before I was; the one was a very great softness and tenderness of heart, which caused me to fall under the conviction of what by Scripture they asserted; and the other was a great bending in my mind to a continual meditating on it, and on all other good things which at any time I heard or read of.

42. By these things my mind was now so turned, that it

lay like a horse leech at the vein, still crying out, Give, give (*Prov. xxx.* 15); yea, it was so fixed on eternity, and on the things about the kingdom of heaven, that is, so far as I knew, though as yet, God knows, I knew but little; that neither pleasures, nor profits, nor persuasions, nor threats, could loosen it, or make it let go his hold; and though I may speak it with shame, yet it is in very deed a certain truth, it would then have been as difficult for me to have taken my mind from heaven to earth, as I have found it often since to get it again from earth to heaven.

43. One thing I may not omit: There was a young man in our town, to whom my heart before was knit more than to any other, but he being a most wicked creature for cursing, and swearing, and whoring, I now shook him off, and forsook his company; but about a quarter of a year after I had left him, I met him in a certain lane, and asked him how he did; he, after his old swearing and mad way, answered, He was well. But, Harry, said I, why do you swear and curse thus? What will become of you, if you die in this condition? He answered me in a great chafe, What would the devil do for company, if it were not for such as I am?

44. About this time I met with some Ranters' books, that were put forth by some of our countrymen, which books were also highly in esteem by several old professors; some of these I read, but was not able to make a judgment about them; wherefore as I read in them, and thought upon them, feeling myself unable to judge, I should betake myself to hearty prayer in this manner: O Lord, I am a fool, and not able to know the truth from error: Lord, leave me not to my own blindness, either to approve of, or condemn this doctrine; if it be of God, let me not despise it; if it be of the devil, let me not embrace it. Lord, I lay my soul, in this matter, only at thy foot; let me not be deceived, I humbly beseech thee. I had one religious intimate companion all this while, and that was the poor man that I spoke of before; but about this time he also turned a most devilish Ranter, and gave himself up to all manner of filthiness, especially uncleanness; he would also deny that there was a God, angel, or spirit;

and would laugh at all exhortations to sobriety. When I laboured to rebuke his wickedness, he would laugh the more, and pretend that he had gone through all religions, and could never light on the right till now. He told me also, that in a little time I should see all professors turn to the ways of the Ranters. Wherefore, abominating those cursed principles, I left his company forthwith, and became to him as great a stranger, as I had been before a familiar.

45. Neither was this man only a temptation to me; but my calling lying in the country, I happened to light into several people's company, who, though strict in religion formerly, yet were also swept away by these Ranters. These would also talk with me of their ways, and condemn me as legal and dark; pretending that they only had attained to perfection that could do what they would, and not sin. Oh! these temptations were suitable to my flesh, I being but a young man, and my nature in its prime; but God, who had, as I hope, designed me for better things, kept me in the fear of his name, and did not suffer me to accept of such principles. And blessed be God, who put it into my heart to cry to him to be kept and directed, still distrusting mine own wisdom; for I have since seen even the effect of that prayer, in his preserving me not only from ranting errors, but from those also that have sprung up since. The Bible was precious to me in those days.

46. And now, methought, I began to look into the Bible with new eyes, and read as I never did before; and especially the epistles of the apostle Paul were sweet and pleasant to me; and, indeed, I was then never out of the Bible, either by reading or meditation; still crying out to God, that I might know the truth, and way to heaven and glory.

47. And as I went on and read, I lighted on that passage, "To one is given by the Spirit the word of wisdom; to another the word of knowledge by the same Spirit; *and* to another faith," etc. (*1 Cor. xii. 8, 9*). And though, as I have since seen, that by this Scripture the Holy Ghost intends, in special, things extraordinary, yet

on me it did then fasten with conviction, that I did want things ordinary, even that understanding and wisdom that other Christians had. On this word I mused, and could not tell what to do, especially this word faith put me to it, for I could not help it, but sometimes must question, whether I had any faith or no; for I feared that it shut me out of all the blessings that other good people had given them of God; but I was loath to conclude I had no faith in my soul; for if I do so, thought I, then I shall count myself a very castaway indeed.

48. No, said I with myself, though I am convinced that I am an ignorant sot, and that I want those blessed gifts of knowledge and understanding that other good people have; yet, at a venture, I will conclude I am not altogether faithless, though I know not what faith is. For it was showed me, and that too, as I have since seen, by Satan, that those who conclude themselves in a faithless state, have neither rest nor quiet in their souls; and I was loath to fall quite into despair.

49. Wherefore, by this suggestion, I was for a while made afraid to see my want of faith; but God would not suffer me thus to undo and destroy my soul, but did continually, against this my blind and sad conclusion, create still within me such suppositions, insomuch that I might in this deceive myself, that I could not rest content, until I did now come to some certain knowledge, whether I had faith or no; this always running in my mind, But how if you want faith indeed? But how can you tell you have faith? And, besides, I saw for certain, if I had not, I was sure to perish for ever.

50. So that though I endeavoured at the first to look over the business of faith, yet in a little time, I better considering the matter, was willing to put myself upon the trial, whether I had faith or no. But, alas, poor wretch, so ignorant and brutish was I, that I knew to this day no more how to do it, than I know how to begin and accomplish that rare and curious piece of art which I never yet saw nor considered.

51. Wherefore, while I was thus considering, and being put to my plunge about it, for you must know, that as yet

I had in this matter broken my mind to no man, only did hear and consider, the tempter came in with his delusion, That there was no way for me to know I had faith, but by trying to work some miracle; urging those Scriptures that seem to look that way, for the enforcing and strengthening his temptation. Nay, one day as I was betwixt Elstow and Bedford, the temptation was hot upon me to try if I had faith, by doing of some miracle: which miracle at that time was this, I must say to the puddles that were in the horse pads, Be dry; and to the dry places, Be you the puddles. And truly, one time I was a-going to say so indeed; but just as I was about to speak, this thought came into my mind, But go under yonder hedge and pray first, that God would make you able. But when I had concluded to pray, this came hot upon me, That if I prayed, and came again and tried to do it, and yet did nothing notwithstanding, then be sure I had no faith, but was a castaway and lost. Nay, thought I, if it be so, I will never try yet, but will stay a little longer.

52. So I continued at a great loss; for I thought, if they only had faith, which could do so wonderful things, then I concluded, that, for the present, I neither had it, nor yet, for time to come, were ever like to have it. Thus I was tossed betwixt the devil and my own ignorance, and so perplexed, especially at some times, that I could not tell what to do.

53. About this time, the state and happiness of these poor people at Bedford was thus, in a dream or vision, represented to me. I saw, as if they were set on the sunny side of some high mountain, there refreshing themselves with the pleasant beams of the sun, while I was shivering and shrinking in the cold, afflicted with frost, snow, and dark clouds. Methought, also, betwixt me and them, I saw a wall that did compass about this mountain; now, through this wall my soul did greatly desire to pass; concluding, that if I could, I would go even into the very midst of them, and there also comfort myself with the heart of their sun.

54. About this wall I thought myself, to go again and again, still prying as I went, to see if I could find some

way or passage, by which I might enter therein; but none could I find for some time. At the last, I saw, as it were, a narrow gap, like a little doorway in the wall, through which I attempted to pass; but the passage being very strait and narrow, I made many efforts to get in, but all in vain, even until I was well-nigh quite beat out, by striving to get in; at last, with great striving, methought I at first did get in my head, and after that, by sidling striving, may shoulders, and my whole body; then was I exceeding glad, and went and sat down in the midst of them, and so was comforted with the light and heat of their sun.

55. Now, this mountain and wall, etc., was thus made out to me—the mountain signified the church of the living God; the sun that shone thereon, the comfortable shining of his merciful face on them that were therein; the wall, I thought, was the Word, that did make separation between the Christians and the world; and the gap which was in this wall, I thought, was Jesus Christ, who is the way to God the Father (*John xiv. 6, Matt. vii. 14*). But forasmuch as the passage was wonderful narrow, even so narrow, that I could not, but with great difficulty, enter in thereat, it showed me that none could enter into life, but those that were in downright earnest, and unless also they left this wicked world behind them; for here was only room for body and soul, but not for body and soul, and sin.

56. This resemblance abode upon my spirit many days; all which time I saw myself in a forlorn and sad condition, but yet was provoked to a vehement hunger and desire to be one of that number that did sit in the sunshine. Now also I should pray wherever I was, whether at home or abroad, in house or field, and should also often, with lifting up of heart, sing that of the 51st Psalm, *O Lord, consider my distress*; for as yet I knew not where I was.

57. Neither as yet could I attain to any comfortable persuasion that I had faith in Christ; but instead of having satisfaction, here I began to find my soul to be assaulted with fresh doubts about my future happiness;

especially with such as these, Whether I was elected? But how, if the day of grace should now be past and gone?

58. By these two temptations I was very much afflicted and disquieted; sometimes by one, and sometimes by the other of them. And first, to speak of that about my questioning my election, I found at this time, that though I was in a flame to find the way to heaven and glory, and though nothing could beat me off from this, yet this question did so offend and discourage me, that I was, especially at some times, as if the very strength of my body also had been taken away by the force and power thereof. This scripture did also seem to me to trample upon all my desires, "*It is* not of him that willeth, nor of him that runneth, but of God that sheweth mercy" (*Rom. ix. 16*).

59. With this scripture I could not tell what to do; for I evidently saw, that unless the great God, of his infinite grace and bounty, had voluntarily chosen me to be a vessel of mercy, though I should desire, and long and labour until my heart did break, no good could come of it. Therefore, this would still stick with me, How can you tell that you are elected? And what if you should not? How then?

60. O Lord, thought I, what if I should not, indeed? It may be you are not, said the tempter; it may be so, indeed, thought I. Why, then, said Satan, you had as good leave off, and strive no further; for if, indeed, you should not be elected and chosen of God, there is no talk of your being saved; "For *it is* neither of him that willeth, nor of him that runneth, but of God that sheweth mercy."

61. By these things I was driven to my wits' end, not knowing what to say, or how to answer these temptations. Indeed, I little thought that Satan had thus assaulted me, but that rather it was my own prudence, thus to start the question; for, that the elect only attained eternal life, that I, without scruple, did heartily close withal; but that myself was one of them, there lay all the question.

62. Thus, therefore, for several days, I was greatly

assaulted and perplexed, and was often, when I have been walking, ready to sink where I went, with faintness in my mind; but one day, after I had been so many weeks oppressed and cast down therewith, as I was now quite giving up the ghost of all my hopes of ever attaining life, that sentence fell with weight upon my spirit, "Look at the generations of old and see; did ever any trust in the Lord, and was confounded?"

63. At which I was greatly lightened and encouraged in my soul; for thus, at that very instant, it was expounded to me, Begin at the beginning of Genesis, and read to the end of the Revelations, and see if you can find that there was ever any that trusted in the Lord, and was confounded. So, coming home, I presently went to my Bible to see if I could find that saying, not doubting but to find it presently; for it was so fresh, and with such strength and comfort on my spirit, that I was as if it talked with me.

64. Well, I looked, but I found it not; only it abode upon me; then I did ask first this good man, and then another, if they knew where it was, but they knew no such place. At this I wondered that such a sentence should so suddenly, and with such comfort and strength, seize and abide upon my heart, and yet that none could find it, for I doubted not but it was in holy Scripture.

65. Thus I continued above a year, and could not find the place; but at last, casting my eye into the Apocrypha books, I found it in *Ecclesiasticus ii. 10*. This, at the first, did somewhat daunt me; but because, by this time, I had got more experience of the love and kindness of God, it troubled me the less; especially when I considered, that though it was not in those texts that we call holy and canonical, yet forasmuch as this sentence was the sum and substance of many of the promises, it was my duty to take the comfort of it; and I bless God for that word, for it was of God to me: that word doth still, at times, shine before my face.

66. After this, that other doubt did come with strength upon me, But how if the day of grace should be past and gone? How if you have overstood the time of mercy?

Now, I remember that one day, as I was walking into the country, I was much in the thoughts of this, But how if the day of grace be past? And to aggravate my trouble, the tempter presented to my mind those good people of Bedford, and suggested thus unto me, That these being converted already, they were all that God would save in those parts; and that I came too late, for these had got the blessing before I came.

67. Now was I in great distress, thinking in very deed that this might well be so; wherefore I went up and down bemoaning my sad condition, counting myself far worse than a thousand fools, for standing off thus long, and spending so many years in sin as I had done; still crying out, Oh, that I had turned sooner! Oh, that I had turned seven years ago! It made me also angry with myself, to think that I should have no more wit, but to trifle away my time till my soul and heaven were lost.

68. But when I had been long vexed with this fear, and was scarce able to take one step more, just about the same place where I received my other encouragement, these words broke in upon my mind, "Compel them to come in, that my house may be filled"; "and yet there is room" (*Luke xiv. 22, 23*). These words, but especially them, "And yet there is room," were sweet words to me; for, truly, I thought that by them I saw there was place enough in heaven for me; and, moreover, that when the Lord Jesus did speak these words, he then did think of me; and that he knowing that the time would come that I should be afflicted with fear that there was no place left for me in his bosom, did before speak this word, and leave it upon record, that I might find help thereby against this vile temptation. This, I then verily believed.

69. In the light and encouragement of this word, I went a pretty while; and the comfort was the more, when I thought that the Lord Jesus should think on me so long ago, and that he should speak them words on purpose for my sake; for I did then think, verily, that he did on purpose speak them, to encourage me withal.

70. But I was not without my temptations to go back again; temptations, I say, both from Satan, mine own

heart, and carnal acquaintance; but I thank God these were outweighed by that sound sense of death and of the day of judgment, which abode, as it were, continually in my view; I should often also think on Nebuchadnezzar, of whom it is said, He had given him all the kingdoms of the earth (*Dan. v. 19*). Yet, thought I, if this great man had all his portion in this world, one hour in hell fire would make him forget all. Which consideration was a great help to me.

71. I was almost made, about this time, to see some thing concerning the beasts that Moses counted clean and unclean. I thought those beasts were types of men; the clean, types of them that were the people of God; but the unclean, types of such as were the children of the wicked one. Now, I read that the clean beasts chewed the cud; that is, thought I, they show us we must feed upon the Word of God. They also parted the hoof; I thought that signified we must part, if we would be saved, with the ways of ungodly men. And also, in further reading about them I found that though we did chew the cud as the hare, yet if we walked with claws like a dog, or if we did part the hoof like the swine, yet if we did not chew the cud as the sheep, we were still, for all that, but unclean; for I thought the hare to be a type of those that talk of the Word, yet walk in the ways of sin; and that the swine was like him that parteth with his outward pollutions, but still wanteth the Word of faith, without which there could be no way of salvation, let a man be never so devout (*Deut. xiv.*). After this I found, by reading the Word, that those that must be glorified with Christ in another world must be called by him here; called to the partaking of a share in his Word and righteousness, and to the comforts and first fruits of his Spirit, and to a peculiar interest in all those heavenly things which do indeed fore fit the soul for that rest and house of glory which is in heaven above.

72. Here, again, I was at a very great stand, not knowing what to do, fearing I was not called; for, thought I, if I be not called, what then can do me good? None but those who are effectually called, inherit the

kingdom of heaven. But oh! how I now loved those words that spake of a Christian's calling! as when the Lord said to one, "Follow me," and to another, "Come after me." And oh! thought I, that he would say so to me too, how gladly would I run after him!

73. I cannot now express with what longings and breakings in my soul I cried to Christ to call me. Thus I continued for a time, all on a flame to be converted to Jesus Christ; and did also see at that day, such glory in a converted state, that I could not be contented without a share therein. Gold! could it have been gotten for gold, what could I have given for it! had I had a whole world it had all gone ten thousand times over for this, that my soul might have been in a converted state.

74. How lovely now was everyone in my eyes that I thought to be converted men and women! they shone, they walked like a people that carried the broad seal of heaven about them. Oh! I saw the lot was fallen to them in pleasant places, and they had a goodly heritage (*Ps. xvi. 6*). But that which made me sick was that of Christ, in Mark, He went up into a mountain and called to him whom he would, and they came unto him (*Mark iii. 13*).

75. This scripture made me faint and fear, yet it kindled fire in my soul. That which made me fear was this, lest Christ should have no liking to me, for he called "whom he would." But oh! the glory that I saw in that condition did still so engage my heart that I could seldom read of any that Christ did call but I presently wished, Would I had been in their clothes; would I had been born Peter; would I had been born John; or would I had been by and had heard him when he called them, how would I have cried, O Lord, call me also. But oh! I feared he would not call me.

76. And truly the Lord let me go thus many months together and showed me nothing; either that I was already, or should be called hereafter. But at last, after much time spent, and many groans to God, that I might be made partaker of the holy and heavenly calling, that Word came in upon me: "I will cleanse their blood *that* I have not cleansed: for the Lord dwelleth in Zion" (*Joel iii.*

21). These words I thought were sent to encourage me to wait still upon God, and signified unto me, that if I were not already, yet time might come I might be in truth converted unto Christ.

77. About this time I began to break my mind to those poor people in Bedford, and to tell them my condition, which, when they had heard, they told Mr. Gifford of me, who himself also took occasion to talk with me, and was willing to be well persuaded of me, though I think but from little grounds: but he invited me to his house, where I should hear him confer with others, about the dealings of God with the soul; from all which I still received more conviction, and from that time began to see something of the vanity and inward wretchedness of my wicked heart, for as yet I knew no great matter therein; but now it began to be discovered unto me, and also to work at that rate for wickedness as it never did before. Now I evidently found that lusts and corruptions would strongly put forth themselves within me, in wicked thoughts and desires, which I did not regard before; my desires also for heaven and life began to fail. I found also, that whereas before my soul was full of longing after God, now my heart began to hanker after every foolish vanity; yea, my heart would not be moved to mind that that was good; it began to be careless, both of my soul and heaven; it would now continually hand back, both to, and in every duty; and was as a clog on the leg of a bird to hinder her from flying.

78. Nay, thought I, now I grow worse and worse; now am I farther from conversion than ever I was before. Wherefore I began to sink greatly in my soul, and began to entertain such discouragement in my heart as laid me low as hell. If now I should have burned at a stake, I could not believe that Christ had love for me; alas, I could neither hear him, nor see him, nor feel him, nor savour any of his things; I was driven as with a tempest, my heart would be unclean, the Canaanites would dwell in the land.

79. Sometimes I would tell my condition to the people of God, which, when they heard, they would pity me,

and would tell me of the promises; but they had as good have told me that I must reach the sun with my finger as have bidden me receive or rely upon the promise; and as soon as I should have done it, all my sense and feeling was against me; and I saw I had a heart that would sin, and that lay under a law that would condemn.

80. These things have often made me think of that child which the father brought to Christ, who, while he was yet a-coming to him, was thrown down by the devil, and also so rent and torn by him that he lay and wallowed, foaming (*Luke ix. 42, Mark ix. 20*).

81. Further, in these days I should find my heart to shut itself up against the Lord, and against his holy Word. I have found my unbelief to set, as it were, the shoulder to the door to keep him out, and that too even then, when I have with many a bitter sigh cried, Good Lord, break it open; Lord, break these gates of brass, and cut these bars of iron asunder (*Ps. cvii. 16*). Yet that word would sometimes create in my heart a peaceable pause, "I girded thee, though thou hast not known me" (*Is. xiv. 5*).

82. But all this while as to the act of sinning, I never was more tender than now; I durst not take a pin or a stick, though but so big as a straw, for my conscience now was sore, and would smart at every touch; I could not now tell how to speak my words, for fear I should misplace them. Oh, how gingerly did I then go in all I did or said! I found myself as on a miry bog that shook If I did but stir; and was there left both of God and Christ, and the Spirit, and all good things.

83. But, I observe, though I was such a great sinner before conversion, yet God never much charged the guilt of the sins of my ignorance upon me; only he showed me I was lost if I had not Christ, because I had been a sinner; I saw that I wanted a perfect righteousness to present me without fault before God, and this righteousness was nowhere to be found, but in the person of Jesus Christ.

84. But my original and inward pollution, that, that was my plague and my affliction; that, I say, at a

dreadful rate, always putting forth itself within me; that I had the guilt of, to amazement; by reason of that, I was more loathsome in my own eyes than was a toad; and I thought I was so in God's eyes too; sin and corruption, I said, would as naturally bubble out of my heart, as water would bubble out of a fountain. I thought now that everyone had a better heart than I had; I could have changed heart with anybody; I thought none but the devil himself could equalise me for inward wickedness and pollution of mind. I fell, therefore, at the sight of my own vileness, deeply into despair; for I concluded that this condition that I was in could not stand with a state of grace. Sure, thought I, I am forsaken of God; sure I am given up to the devil, and to a reprobate mind; and thus I continued a long while, even for some years together.

85. While I was thus afflicted with the fears of my own damnation, there were two things would make me wonder; the one was, when I saw old people hunting after the things of this life, as if they should live here always; the other was, when I found professors much distressed and cast down, when they met with outward losses; as of husband, wife, child, etc. Lord, thought I, what ado is here about such little things as these! What seeking after carnal things by some, and what grief in others for the loss of them! If they so much labour after, and spend so many tears for the things of this present life, how am I to be bemoaned, pitied, and prayed for! My soul is dying, my soul is damning. Were my soul but in a good condition, and where I but sure of it, oh! how rich should I esteem myself, though blessed but with bread and water; I should count those but small afflictions, and should bear them as little burdens. "A wounded spirit who can bear?"

86. And though I was thus troubled, and tossed, and afflicted, with the sight and sense and terror of my own wickedness, yet I was afraid to let this sight and sense go quite off my mind; for I found, that unless guilt of conscience was taken off the right way, that is, by the blood of Christ, a man grew rather worse for the loss of

his trouble of mind, than better. Wherefore, if my guilt lay hard upon me, then I should cry that the blood of Christ might take it off; and if it was going off without it (for the sense of sin would be sometimes as if it would die, and go quite away), then I would also strive to fetch it upon my heart again, by bringing the punishment for sin in hell fire upon my spirits; and should cry. Lord, let it not go off my heart, but the right way, but by the blood of Christ, and by the application of thy mercy, through him, to my soul; for that scripture lay much upon me, "without shedding of blood is no remission" (*Heb. ix. 22*). And that which made me the more afraid of this was, because I had seen some who, though when they were under wounds of conscience, then they would cry and pray; but they seeking rather present ease from their trouble, than pardon for their sin, cared not how they lost their guilt, so they got it out of their mind; and, therefore, having got it off the wrong way, it was nor sanctified unto them; but they grew harder and blinder, and more wicked after their trouble. This made me afraid, and made me cry to God the more, that it might not be so with me.

87. And now was I sorry that God had made me a man, for I feared I was a reprobate; I counted man as unconverted, the most doleful of all the creatures. Thus being afflicted and tossed about my sad condition, I counted myself alone, and above the most of men unblessed.

88. Yea, I thought it impossible that ever I should attain to so much goodness of heart, as to thank God that he had made me a man. Man indeed is the most noble by creation, of all creatures in the visible world; but by sin he had made himself the most ignoble. The beasts, birds, fishes, etc., I blessed their condition, for they had not a sinful nature, they were not obnoxious to the wrath of God; they were not to go to hell fire after death; I could therefore have rejoiced, had my condition been as any of theirs.

89. In this condition I went a great while; but when comforting time was come, I heard one preach a sermon

upon those words in the Song (*iv. 1*), "Behold, thou *art* fair, my love; behold, thou *art* fair." But at that time he made these two words, "My love," his chief and subject matter; from which, after he had a little opened the text, he observed these several conclusions: 1. That the church, and so every saved soul, is Christ's love, when loveless. 2. Christ's love without a cause. 3. Christ's love when hated of the world. 4. Christ's love when under temptation, and under desertion. 5. Christ's love from first to last.

90. But I got nothing by what he said at present, only when he came to the application of the fourth particular, this was the word he said: If it be so, that the saved soul is Christ's love when under temptation and desertion; then, poor tempted soul, when thou art assaulted and afflicted with temptation, and the hidings of God's face, yet think on these two words, "My love," still.

91. So as I was a-going home, these words came again into my thoughts; and I well remember, as they came in, I said thus in my heart, What shall I get by thinking on these two words? This thought had no sooner passed through my heart, but the words began thus to kindle in my spirit, "Thou art my love, thou art my love," twenty times together; and still as they ran thus in my mind, they waxed stronger and warmer, and began to make me look up; but being as yet between hope and fear, I still replied in my heart, But is it true, but is it true? At which, that sentence fell in upon me, He "wist not that it was true which was done by the angel" (*Acts xii. 9*).

92. Then I began to give place to the word, which, with power, did over and over make this joyful sound within my soul, Thou art my love, thou art my love; and nothing shall separate thee from my love; and with that, *Rom. viii. 36* came into my mind. Now was my heart filled full of comfort and hope, and now I could believe that my sins should be forgiven me; yea, I was now so taken with the love and mercy of God, that I remember I could not tell how to contain till I got home; I thought I could have spoken of his love, and of his mercy to me, even to the very crows that sat upon the ploughed lands before me,

had they been capable to have understood me; wherefore I said in my soul, with much gladness, Well, I would I had a pen and ink here, I would write this down before I go any farther, for surely I will not forget this forty years hence; but alas! within less than forty days, I began to question all again; which made me begin to question all still.

93. Yet still at times, I was helped to believe that it was a true manifestation of grace unto my soul, though I had lost much of the life and savour of it. Now about a week or fortnight after this, I was much followed by this scripture, "Simon, Simon, behold, Satan hath desired *to have* you" (*Luke xxiii. 31*). And sometimes it would sound so loud within me, yea, and as it were call so strongly after me, that once above all the rest, I turned my head over my shoulder, thinking verily that some man had, behind me, called to me; being at a great distance, methought he called so loud; it came, as I have thought since, to have stirred me up to prayer, and to watchfulness; it came to acquaint me that a cloud and a storm was coming down upon me, but I understood it not.

94. Also, as I remember, that time that it called to me so loud, was the last time that it sounded in mine ear; but methinks I hear still with what a loud voice these words, Simon, Simon, sounded in mine ears. I thought verily, as I have told you, that somebody had called after me, that was half a mile behind me; and although that was not my name, yet it made me suddenly look behind me, believing that he that called so loud meant me.

95. But so foolish was I, and ignorant, that I knew not the reason of this sound; which, as I did both see and feel soon after, was sent from heaven as an alarm, to awaken me to provide for what was coming; only it would make me muse and wonder in my mind, to think what should be the reason that this scripture, and that at this rate, so often and so loud, should still be sounding and rattling in mine ears; but, as I said before, I soon after perceived the end of God therein.

96. For about the space of a month after, a very great storm came down upon me, which handled me twenty

times worse than all I had met with before; it came stealing upon me, now by one piece, then by another; first, all my comfort was taken from me, then darkness seized upon me, after which whole floods of blasphemies, both against God, Christ, and the Scriptures, were poured upon my spirit, to my great confusion and astonishment. These blasphemous thoughts were such as also stirred up questions in me, against the very being of God, and of his only beloved Son; as, whether they were, in truth, a God, or Christ, or no? And whether the holy Scriptures were not rather a fable, and cunning story, then the holy and pure Word of God?

97. The tempter would also much assault me with this, How can you tell but that the Turks had as good Scriptures to prove their Mahomet the Saviour, as we have to prove our Jesus is? And, could I think, that so many ten thousands, in so many countries and kingdoms, should be without the knowledge of the right way to heaven; if there were indeed a heaven, and that we only, who live in a corner of the earth, should alone be blessed therewith? Everyone doth think his own religion rightest, both Jews and Moors, and Pagans! and how if all our faith, and Christ, and Scriptures, should be but a think-so too?

98. Sometimes I have endeavoured to argue against these suggestions, and to set some of the sentences of blessed Paul against them; but, alas! I quickly felt, when I thus did, such arguings as these would return again upon me, Though we made so great a matter of Paul, and of his words, yet how could I tell, but that in very deed, he being a subtle and cunning man, might give himself up to deceive with strong delusions; and also take both that pains and travail, to undo and destroy his fellows?

99. These suggestions, with many other which at this time I may not, nor dare not utter, neither by word not pen, did make such a seizure upon my spirit, and did so overweigh my heart, both with their number, continuance, and fiery force, that I felt as if there were nothing else but these from morning to night within me;

and as though, indeed, there could be room for nothing else; and also concluded that God had, in very wrath to my soul, given me up unto them, to be carried away with them, as with a mighty whirlwind.

100. Only by the distaste that they gave unto my spirit, I felt there was something in me that refused to embrace them. But this consideration I then only had, when God gave me leave to swallow my spittle, otherwise the noise, and strength, and force of these temptations, would drown and overflow; and as it were, bury all such thoughts or the remembrance of any such thing. While I was in this temptation, I should often find my mind suddenly put upon it, to curse and swear, or to speak some grievous thing against God, or Christ his Son, and of the Scriptures.

101. Now I thought, surely I am possessed of the devil; at other times again, I thought I should be bereft of my wits; for instead of lauding and magnifying God the Lord with others, if I have but heard him spoken of, presently some most horrible blasphemous thought or other would bolt out of my heart against him; so that whether I did think that God was, or again did think there were no such thing, no love, nor peace, nor gracious disposition could I feel within me.

102. These things did sink me into very deep despair; for I concluded, that such things could not possibly be found amongst them that loved God. I often, when these temptations have been with force upon me, did compare myself in the case of such a child, whom some gipsy hath by force took up under her apron, and is carrying from friend and country; kick sometimes I did, and also scream and cry; but yet I was as bound in the wings of the temptation, and the wind would carry me away. I thought also of Saul, and of the evil spirit that did possess him; and did greatly fear that my condition was the same with that of his (*1 Sam. xvi. 14*).

103. In these days, when I have heard others talk of what was the sin against the Holy Ghost, then would the tempter so provoke me to desire to sin that sin, that I was as if I could not, must not, neither should be quiet until I

had committed that; now, no sin would serve but that; if
it were to be committed by speaking of such a word, then
I have been as if my mouth would have spoken that
word, whether I would or no; and in so strong a measure
was this temptation upon me, that often I have been
ready to clap my hand under my chin, to hold my mouth
from opening; and to that end also I have had thoughts
at other times, to leap with my head downward, into
some muck-hill hole or other, to keep my mouth from
speaking.

104. Now I blessed the condition of the dog and toad,
and counted the estate of everything that God had made
far better than this dreadful state of mine, and such as
my companions was; yea, gladly would I have been in
the condition of dog or horse, for I knew they had no soul
to perish under the everlasting weights of hell for sin, as
mine was like to do. Nay, and though I saw this, felt this,
and was broken to pieces with it, yet that which added to
my sorrow was, that I could not find that with all my
soul I did desire deliverance. That scripture did also tear
and rend my soul, in the midst of these distractions,
"The wicked *are* like the troubled sea, when it cannot
rest, whose waters cast up mire and dirt. *There is* no
peace, saith my God, to the wicked" (*Is. lvii. 20, 21*).

105. And now my heart was, at times, exceeding hard;
if I would have given a thousand pounds for a tear, I
could not shed one; no, nor sometimes scarce desire to
shed one. I was much dejected to think that this should
be my lot. I saw some could mourn and lament their sin;
and others, again, could rejoice, and bless God for
Christ; and others, again, could quietly talk of, and with
gladness remember, the Word of God; while I only was
in the storm or tempest. This much sunk me; I thought
my condition was alone. I should, therefore, much
bewail my hard hap; but get out of, or get rid of, these
things, I could not.

106. While this temptation lasted, which was about a
year, I could attend upon none of the ordinances of God
but with sore and great affliction. Yea, then was I most
distressed with blasphemies; if I have been hearing the

Word, then uncleanness, blasphemies, and despair would hold me as captive there; if I have been reading, then, sometimes, I had sudden thoughts to question all I read; sometimes, again, my mind would be so strangely snatched away, and possessed with other things, that I have neither known, nor regarded, nor remembered so much as the sentence that but now I have read.

107. In prayer, also, I have been greatly troubled at this time; sometimes I have thought I should see the devil, nay, thought I have felt him, behind me, pull my clothes; he would be, also, continually at me in the time of prayer to have done; break off, make haste, you have prayed enough, and stay no longer, still drawing my mind away. Sometimes, also, he would cast in such wicked thoughts as these: that I must pray to him, or for him. I have thought sometimes of that—Fall down, or, "if thou wilt fall down and worship me" (*Matt. iv. 9*).

108. Also, when, because I have had wandering thoughts in the time of this duty, I have laboured to compose my mind and fix it upon God, then, with great force, hath the tempter laboured to distract me, and confound me, and to turn away my mind, by presenting to my heart and fancy the form of a bush, a bull, a besom, or the like, as if I should pray to those; to these he would, also, at some times especially, so hold my mind that I was as if I could think of nothing else, or pray to nothing else but to these, or such as they.

109. Yet, at times I should have some strong and heart-affecting apprehensions of God, and the reality of the truth of his gospel; but, oh! how would my heart, at such times, put forth itself with inexpressible groanings. My whole soul was then in every word; I should cry with pangs after God that he would be merciful unto me; but then I should be daunted again with such conceits as these; I should think that God did mock at these, my prayers, saying, and that in the audience of the holy angels, This poor simple wretch doth hanker after me as if I had nothing to do with my mercy but to bestow it on such as he. Alas, poor fool! how art thou deceived! It is not for such as thee to have favour with the Highest.

110. Then hath the tempter come upon me, also, with such discouragements as these: You are very hot for mercy, but I will cool you; this frame shall not last always; many have been as hot as you for a spirit, but I have quenched their zeal. And with this, such and such who were fallen off would be set before mine eyes. Then I should be afraid that I should do so too; but, thought I, I am glad this comes into my mind. Well, I will watch, and take what heed I can. Though you do, said Satan, I shall be too hard for you; I will cool you insensibly, by degrees, by little and little. What care I, saith he, though I be seven years in chilling your heart if I can do it at last? Continual rocking will lull a crying child asleep. I will ply it close, but I will have my end accomplished. Though you be burning hot at present, yet, if I can pull you from this fire, I shall have you cold before it be long.

111. These things brought me into great straits; for as I at present could not find myself fit for present death, so I thought to live long would make me yet more unfit; for time would make me forget all, and wear even the remembrance of the evil of sin, the worth of heaven, and the need I had of the blood of Christ to wash me, both out of mind and thought; but I thank Christ Jesus these things did not at present make me slack my crying, but rather did put me more upon it, like her who met with the adulterer (*Deut. xxii. 27*); in which days that was a good word to me after I had suffered these things a while: "I am persuaded that neither ... height, nor depth, nor life," etc., "shall ... separate us from the love of God, which is in Christ Jesus" (*Rom. viii. 38*). And now I hoped long life should not destroy me, nor make me miss of heaven.

112. Yet I had some supports in this temptation, though they were then all questioned by me; that in the third of Jeremiah, at the first, was something to me, and so was the consideration of the fifth verse of that chapter; that though we have spoken and done as evil things as we could, yet we should cry unto God, "My Father, thou *art* the guide of my youth"; and should return unto him.

113. I had, also, once a sweet glance from that in 2 *Cor,*

v. 21: "For he hath made him *to be* sin for us, who knew no sin; that we might be made the righteousness of God in him." I remember, also, that one day as I was sitting in a neighbour's house, and there very sad at the consideration of my many blasphemies, and as I was saying in my mind, What ground have I to think that I, who have been so vile and abominable, should ever inherit eternal life? that word came suddenly upon me, "What shall we then say to these things? If God *be* for us, who *can be* against us?" (*Rom. viii. 31*). That, also, was an help unto me, "Because I live, ye shall live also" (*John xiv. 19*). But these were but hints, touches, and short visits, though very sweet when present; only they lasted not; but, like to Peter's sheet, of a sudden were caught up from me to heaven again (*Acts x. 16*).

114. But afterwards the Lord did more fully and graciously discover himself unto me; and, indeed, did quite, not only deliver me from the guilt that, by these things, was laid upon my conscience, but also from the very filth thereof; for the temptation was removed, and I was put into my right mind again, as other Christians were.

115. I remember that one day, as I was travelling into the country and musing on the wickedness and blasphemy of my heart, and considering of the enmity that was in me to God, that scripture came in my mind, He hath "made peace through the blood of his cross" (*Col. i. 20*). By which I was made to see, both again, and again, and again, that day, that God and my soul were friends by this blood; yea. I saw that the justice of God and my sinful soul could embrace and kiss each other through this blood. This was a good day to me; I hope I shall not forget it.

116. At another time, as I sat by the fire in my house, and musing on my wretchedness, the Lord made that also a precious word unto me, "Forasmuch, then, as the children are partakers of flesh and blood, he also himself likewise took part of the same; that through death he might destroy him that had the power of death, that is, the devil, and deliver them who, through fear of death,

were all their lifetime subject to bondage" (*Heb. ii. 14, 15*). I thought that the glory of these words was then so weighty on me that I was, both once and twice, ready to swoon as I sat; yet not with grief and trouble, but with solid joy and peace.

117. At this time, also, I sat under the ministry of holy Mr. Gifford, whose doctrine, by God's grace, was much for my stability. This man made it much his business to deliver the people of God from all those faults and unsound rests that, by nature, we are prone to take and make to our souls. He pressed us to take special heed that we took not up any truth upon trust—as from this, or that, or any other man or men—but to cry mightily to God that he would convince us of the reality thereof, and set us down therein, by his own Spirit, in the holy Word; for, said he, if you do otherwise when temptations come, if strongly, you, not having received them with evidence from heaven, will find you want that help and strength now to resist as once you thought you had.

118. This was as seasonable to my soul as the former and latter rain in their season; for I had found, and that by sad experience, the truth of these his words; for I had felt what no man can say, especially when tempted by the devil, that Jesus Christ is Lord but by the Holy Ghost. Wherefore I found my soul, through grace, very apt to drink in this doctrine, and to incline to pray to God that, in nothing that pertained to God's glory and my own eternal happiness, he would suffer me to be without the confirmation thereof from heaven; for now I saw clearly there was an exceeding difference betwixt the notions of flesh and blood, and the revelations of God in heaven; also a great difference between that faith that is feigned, and according to man's wisdom, and of that which comes by a man's being born thereto of God (*Matt. xvi. 15–17; 1 John v. 1*).

119. But, oh! now, how was my soul led from truth to truth by God! even from the birth and cradle of the Son of God to his ascension and second coming from heaven to judge the world.

120. Truly, I then found, upon this account, the great

God was very good unto me; for, to my remembrance, there was not anything that I then cried unto God to make known and reveal unto me but he was pleased to do it for me; I mean not one part of the gospel of the Lord Jesus, but I was orderly led into it. Methought I saw with great evidence, from the relation of the four evangelists, the wonderful work of God, in giving Jesus Christ to save us, from his conception and birth even to his second coming to judgment. Methought I was as if I had seen him born, as if I had seen him grow up, as if I had seen him walk through this world, from the cradle to his cross: to which, also, when he came. I saw how gently he gave himself to be hanged and nailed on it for my sins and wicked doings. Also, as I was musing on this, his progress, that dropped on my spirit, He was ordained for the slaughter (*1 Pet. i. 19, 20*).

121. When I have considered also the truth of his resurrection, and have remembered that word, "Touch me not, Mary," etc., I have seen as if he leaped at the grave's mouth for joy that he was risen again, and had got the conquest over our dreadful foes (*John xx. 17*). I have also, in the spirit, seen him a man on the right hand of God the Father for me, and have seen the manner of his coming from heaven to judge the world with glory, and have been confirmed in these things by these scriptures following, *Acts i. 9, 10; vii. 56; x. 42; Heb. vii. 24; viii. 3; Rev. i. 18; 1 Thess. iv. 17, 18.*

122. Once I was much troubled to know whether the Lord Jesus was both man as well as God, and God as well as man; and truly, in those days, let men say what they would, unless I had it with evidence from heaven, all was as nothing to me, I counted not myself set down in any truth of God. Well, I was much troubled about this point, and could not tell how to be resolved; at last, that in the fifth of the Revelations came into my mind, "And I beheld, and lo, in the midst of the throne and of the four beasts, and in the midst of the elders, stood a Lamb." In the midst of the throne, thought I, there is his Godhead; in the midst of the elders, there is his manhood; but oh! methought this did glister! it was a goodly

touch, and gave me sweet satisfaction. That other scripture also did help me much in this, "To us a child is born, unto us a son is given; and the government shall be upon his shoulder: and his name shall be called Wonderful, Counsellor, The mighty God, The everlasting Father, The Prince of Peace," etc. (*Is. ix. 6*).

123. Also, besides these teachings of God in his World, the Lord made use of two things to confirm me in these things; the one was the errors of the Quakers, and the other was the guilt of sin; for as the Quakers did oppose his truth, so God did the more confirm me in it, by leading me into the scriptures that did wonderfully maintain it.

124. The errors that this people then maintained were: 1. That the holy Scriptures were not the Word of God. 2. That every man in the world had the spirit of Christ, grace, faith, etc. 3. That Christ Jesus, as crucified, and dying 1600 years ago, did not satisfy divine justice for the sins of the people. 4. That Christ's flesh and blood was within the saints. 5. That the bodies of the good and bad that are buried in the churchyard shall not arise again. 6. That the resurrection is past with good men already. 7. That that man Jesus, that was crucified between two thieves on Mount Calvary, in the land of Canaan, by Jerusalem, was not ascended up above the starry heavens. 8. That he should not, even the same Jesus that died by the hands of the Jews, come again at the last day, and as man judge all nations, etc.

125. Many more vile and abominable things were in those days formented by them, by which I was driven to a more narrow search of the Scriptures, and was, through their light and testimony, not only enlightened, but greatly confirmed and comforted in the truth; and, as I said, the guilt of sin did help me much, for still as that would come upon me, the blood of Christ did take it off again, and again, and again, and that too, sweetly, according to the Scriptures. O friends! cry to God to reveal Jesus Christ unto you; there is none teacheth like him.

126. It would be too long for me here to stay, to tell you

in particular how God did set me down in all the things
of Christ, and how he did, that he might so do, lead me
into his words; yea, and also how he did open them unto
me, make them shine before me, and cause them to dwell
with me, talk with me, and comfort me over and over,
both of his own being, and the being of his Son, and
Spirit, and Word, and gospel.

127. Only this, as I said before I will say unto you
again, that in general he was pleased to take this course
with me; first, to suffer me to be afflicted with temptation
concerning them, and then reveal them to me: as sometimes I should lie under great guilt for sin, even crushed
to the ground therewith, and then the Lord would
show me the death of Christ; yea, and so sprinkle my
conscience with his blood, that I should find, and that
before I was aware, that in that conscience where but
just now did reign and rage the law, even there would
rest and abide the peace and love of God through Christ.

128. Now had I an evidence, as I thought, of my
salvation from heaven, with many golden seals thereon,
all hanging in my sight; now could I remember this
manifestation and the other discovery of grace, with
comfort; and should often long and desire that they last
day were come, that I might for ever be inflamed with
the sight, and joy, and communion with him whose head
was crowned with thorns, whose face was spit on, and
body broken, and soul made an offering for my sins: for
whereas, before, I lay continually trembling at the mouth
of hell, now methought I was got so far therefrom that I
could not, when I looked back, scarce discern it; and, oh!
thought I, that I were fourscore years old now, that I
might die quickly, that my soul might be gone to rest.

129. But before I had got thus far out of these my
temptations, I did greatly long to see some ancient godly
man's experience, who had writ some hundreds of years
before I was born; for those who had writ in our days, I
thought, but I desire them now to pardon me, that they
had writ only that which others felt, or else had, through
the strength of their wits and parts, studied to answer
such objections as they perceived others were perplexed

with, without going down themselves into the deep. Well, after many such longings in my mind, the God in whose hands are all our days and ways, did cast into my hand, one day, a book of Martin Luther; it was his comment on the Galatians—it also was so old that it was ready to fall piece from piece if I did but turn it over. Now I was pleased much that such an old book had fallen into my hands; the which, when I had but a little way perused, I found my condition, in his experience, so largely and profoundly handled, as if his book had been written out of my heart. This made me marvel; for thus thought I, This man could not know anything of the state of Christians now, but must needs write and speak the experience of former days.

130. Besides, he doth most gravely, also, in that book, debate of the rise of these temptations, namely, blasphemy, desperation, and the like; showing that the law of Moses as well as the devil, death, and hell hath a very great hand therein, the which, at first, was very strange to me; but considering and watching, I found it so indeed. But of particulars here I intend nothing; only this, methinks, I must let fall before all men, I do prefer this book of Martin Luther upon the Galatians, excepting the Holy Bible, before all the books that ever I have seen, as most fit for a wounded conscience.

131. And now I found, as I thought, that I loved Christ dearly; oh! methought my soul cleaved into him, my affections cleaved unto him. I felt love to him as hot as fire; and now, as Job said, I thought I should die in my nest; but I did quickly find that my great love was but little, and that I, who had, as I thought, such burning love to Jesus Christ, could let him go again for a very trifle; God can tell how to abase us, and can hide pride from man. Quickly after this my love was tried to purpose.

132. For after the Lord had, in this manner, thus graciously delivered me from this great and sore temptation, and had set me down so sweetly in the faith of his holy gospel, and had given me such strong consolation and blessed evidence from heaven touching my interest

in his love through Christ; the tempter came upon me again, and that with a more grievous and dreadful temptation than before.

133. And that was, To sell and part with this most blessed Christ, to exchange him for the things of his life, for anything. The temptation lay upon me for the space of a year, and did follow me so continually that I was not rid of it one day in a month, no, not sometimes one hour in many days together, unless when I was asleep.

134. And though, in my judgment, I was persuaded that those who were once effectually in Christ, as I hoped, through his grace, I had seen myself, could never lose him for ever—for "the land shall not be sold for ever, for the land *is* mine," saith God (*Lev. xxv.23*)—yet it was a continual vexation to me to think that I should have so much as one such thought within me against a Christ, a Jesus, that had done for me as he had done; and yet then I had almost none others, but such blasphemous ones.

135. But it was neither my dislike of the thought, nor yet any desire and endeavour to resist it that in the least did shake or abate the continuation, or force and strength thereof; for it did always, in almost whatever I thought, intermix itself therewith in such sort that I could neither eat my food, stoop for a pin, chop a stick, or cast mine eye to look on this or that, but still the temptation would come, Sell Christ for this, or sell Christ for that; sell him, sell him.

136. Sometimes it would run in my thoughts, not so little as a hundred times together, Sell him, sell him, sell him; against which I may say, for whole hours together, I have been forced to stand as continually learning and forcing my spirit against it, lest haply, before I were aware, some wicked thought might arise in my heart that might consent thereto; and sometimes also the tempter would make me believe I had consented to it, then should I be as tortured upon a rack for whole days together.

137. This temptation did put me to such scares, lest I should at sometimes, I say, consent thereto, and be overcome therewith, that by the very force of my mind,

in labouring to gainsay and resist this wickedness, my very body also would be put into action or motion by way of pushing or thrusting with my hands or elbows, still answering as fast as the destroyer said, Sell him; I will not, I will not, I will not, I will not; no, not for thousands, thousands, thousands of worlds. Thus reckoning lest I should in the midst of these assaults, set too low a value of him, even until I scarce well knew where I was, or how to be composed again.

138. At these seasons he would not let me eat my food at quiet; but, forsooth, when I was set at the table at my meat, I must go hence to pray; I must leave my food now, and just now, so counterfeit holy also would this devil be. When I was thus tempted, I should say in myself, Now I am at my meat, let me make an end. No, said he, you must do it now, or you will displease God, and despise Christ. Wherefore I was much afflicted with these things; and because of the sinfulness of my nature, imagining that these things were impulses from God, I should deny to do it, as if I denied God; and then should I be as guilty, because I did not obey a temptation of the devil, as if I had broken the law of God indeed.

139. But to be brief, one morning, as I did lie in my bed, I was, as at other times, most fiercely assaulted with this temptation, to sell and part with Christ; the wicked suggestion still running in my mind, Sell him, sell him, sell him, sell him, sell him, as fast as a man could speak; against which also, in my mind, as at other times, I answered, No, no, not for thousands, thousands, thousands, at least twenty times together. But at last, after much striving, even until I was almost out of breath, I felt this thought pass through my heart, Let him go, if he will! and I thought also, that I felt my heart freely consent thereto. Oh, the diligence of Satan! Oh, the desperateness of man's heart!

140. Now was the battle won, and down fell I, as a bird that is shot from the top of a tree, into great guilt, and fearful despair. Thus getting out of my bed, I went moping into the field; but God knows, with as heavy a heart as mortal man, I think, could bear; where, for the

space of two hours, I was like a man bereft of life, and as now past all recovery, and bound over to eternal punishment.

141. And withal, that scripture did seize upon my soul, "Or profane person, as Esau, who for one morsel of meat, sold his birthright; for ye know, how that afterward, when he would have inherited the blessing, he was rejected; for he found no place of repentance, though he sought it carefully with tears" (*Heb. xii. 16, 17*).

142. Now was I as one bound, I felt myself shut up unto the judgment to come; nothing now for two years together would abide with me, but damnation, and an expectation of damnation; I say, nothing now would abide with me but this, save some few moments for relief, as in the sequel you will see.

143. These words were to my soul like fetters of brass to my legs, in the continual sound of which I went for several months together. But about ten or eleven o'clock one day, as I was walking under a hedge, full of sorrow and guilt, God knows, and bemoaning myself for this hard hap, that such a thought should arise within me; suddenly this sentence bolted in upon me, The blood of Christ remits all guilt. At this I made a stand in my spirit; with that, this word took hold upon me, "The blood of Jesus Christ, his Son, cleanseth us from all sin" (*1 John i. 7*).

144. Now I began to conceive peace in my soul, and methought I saw as if the tempter did leer and steal away from me, as being ashamed of what he had done. At the same time also I had my sin, and the blood of Christ thus represented to me, that my sin, when compared to the blood of Christ, was no more to it, than this little clot or stone before me, is to this vast and wide field that here I see. This gave me good encouragement for the space of two or three hours; in which time also, methought I saw, by faith, the Son of God, as suffering for my sins; but because it tarried not, I therefore sunk in my spirit, under exceeding guilt again.

145. But chiefly by the afore-mentioned scripture, concerning Esau's selling of his birthright; for that

scripture would lie all day long, all the week long, yea, all
the year long in my mind, and hold me down, so that I
could by no means lift up myself; for when I would strive
to turn me to this scripture, or that, for relief, still that
sentence would be sounding in me, "For ye know, how
that afterward, when he would have inherited the
blessing ... he found no place of repentance, though he
sought it carefully with tears."

146. Sometimes, also, I should have a touch from that
in *Luke xxii. 32*, "I have prayed for thee, that thy faith fail
not"; but it would not abide upon me; neither could I
indeed, when I considered my state, find ground to
conceive in the least, that there should be the root
of that grace within me, having sinned as I had done.
Now was I torn and rent in heavy case, for many days
together.

147. Then began I with sad and careful heart, to
consider of the nature and largeness of my sin, and to
search in the Word of God, if I could in any place espy a
word of promise, or any encouraging sentence by which I
might take relief. Wherefore I began to consider that
third of Mark, All manner of sins and blasphemies shall
be forgiven unto the sons of men, wherewith soever they
shall blaspheme. Which place, methought, at a blush,
did contain a large and glorious promise, for the pardon
of high offences; but considering the place more fully, I
thought it was rather to be understood as relating more
chiefly to those who had, while in a natural estate,
committed such things as there are mentioned; but not to
me, who had not only received light and mercy, but that
had, both after, and also contrary to that, so slighted
Christ as I had done.

148. I feared therefore that this wicked sin of mine
might be that sin unpardonable, of which he there thus
speaketh, "But he that shall blaspheme against the Holy
Ghost hath never forgiveness, but is in danger of eternal
damnation" (*Mark, iii. 29*). And I did the rather give
credit to this, because of that sentence in the Hebrews,
"For ye know, how that afterward, when he would have
inherited the blessing, he was rejected; for he found no

place of repentance, though he sought it carefully with tears." And this stuck always with me.

149. And now was I both a burden and a terror to myself, nor did I ever so know, as now, what it was to be weary of my life, and yet afraid to die. Oh, how gladly now would I have been anybody but myself! Anything but a man! and in any condition but mine own! for there was nothing did pass more frequently over my mind, than that it was impossible for me to be forgiven my transgression, and to be saved from wrath to come.

150. And now began I to labour to call again time that was past; wishing a thousand times twice told, that the day was yet to come, when I should be tempted to such a sin; concluding with great indignation, both against my heart, and all assaults, how I would rather have been torn in pieces, than found a consenter thereto. But, alas! these thoughts, and wishings, and resolvings, were now too late to help me; the thought had passed my heart, God hath let me go, and I am fallen. Oh! thought I, "that it was with me as in months past, as in the days *when* God preserved me!" (*Job xxix. 2*).

151. Then again, being loath and unwilling to perish, I began to compare my sin with others, to see if I could find that any of those that were saved had done as I had done. So I considered David's adultery and murder, and found them most heinous crimes; and those too committed after light and grace received; but yet by considering, I perceived that his transgressions were only such as were against the law of Moses; from which the Lord Christ could, with the consent of his Word, deliver him: but mine was against the gospel; yea, against the Mediator thereof; I had sold my Saviour.

152. Now again should I be as if racked upon the wheel, when I considered, that, besides the guilt that possessed me, I should be so void of grace, so bewitched. What, thought I, must it be no sin but this? Must it needs be the *great transgression* (*Ps. xix. 13*)? Must *that* wicked one touch my soul (*1 John v. 18*)? Oh, what stings did I find in all these sentences!

153. What, thought I, is there but one sin that is

unpardonable? But one sin that layeth the soul without the reach of God's mercy; and must I be guilty of that? Must it needs be that? Is there but one sin among so many millions of sins, for which there is no forgiveness; and must I commit this? Oh, unhappy sin! Oh, unhappy man! These things would so break and confound my spirit, that I could not tell what to do; I thought, at times, they would have broke my wits; and still, to aggravate my misery, that would run in my mind, "Ye know how that afterward, when he would have inherited the blessing, he was rejected." Oh! none knows the terrors of those days but myself.

154. After this I came to consider of Peter's sin, which he committed in denying his master; and indeed, this came nighest to mine, of any that I could find; for he had denied his Saviour, as I, and that after light and mercy received; yea, and that too, after warning given him. I also considered, that he did it both once and twice; and that, after time to consider betwixt. But though I put all these circumstances together, that, if possible, I might find help, yet I considered again, that his was but a denial of his master, but mine was a selling of my Saviour. Wherefore I thought with myself, that I came nearer to Judas, than either to David or Peter.

155. Here again my torment would flame out and afflict me; yea, it would grind me, as it were, to powder, to discern the preservation of God towards others, while I fell into the snare; for in my thus considering of other men's sins, and comparing of them with my own, I could evidently see how God preserved them, notwithstanding their wickedness, and would not let them, as he had let me, to become a son of perdition.

156. But oh, how did my soul, at this time, prize the preservation that God did set about his people! Ah, how safely did I see them walk, whom God had hedged in! They were within his care, protection, and special providence; though they were full as bad as I by nature; yet because he loved them, he would not suffer them to fall without the range of mercy; but as for me, I was gone, I had done it; he would not preserve me, nor keep

me; but suffered me, because I was a reprobate, to fall as I had done. Now, did those blessed places, that spake of God's keeping his people, shine like the sun before me, though not to comfort me, but to show me the blessed state and heritage of those whom the Lord had blessed.

157. Now I saw, that as God had his hand in all providences and dispensations that overtook his elect, so he had his hand in all the temptations that they had to sin against him, not to animate them unto wickedness, but to choose their temptations and troubles for them; and also to leave them, for a time, to such sins only as might not destroy, but humble them; as might not put them beyond, but lay them in the way of the renewing of his mercy. But oh, what love, what care, what kindness and mercy did I now see, mixing itself with the most severe and dreadful of all God's ways to his people! He would let David, Hezekiah, Solomon, Peter, and others fall, but he would not let them fall into sin unpardonable, nor into hell for sin. Oh! thought I, these be the men that God hath loved; these be the men that God, though he chastiseth them, keeps them in safety by him, and them whom he makes to abide under the shadow of the Almighty. But all these thoughts added sorrow, grief, and horror to me, as whatever I now thought on, it was killing to me. If I thought how God kept his own that was killing to me. If I thought of how I was falling myself, that was killing to me. As all things wrought together for the best, and to do good to them that were the called, according to his purpose; so I thought that all things wrought for my damage, and for my eternal overthrow.

158. Then, again, I began to compare my sin with the sin of Judas, that, if possible, I might find that mine differed from that which, in truth, is unpardonable. And, oh! thought I, if it should differ from it, though but the breadth of an hair, what a happy condition is my soul in! And, by considering, I found that Judas did his intentionally, but mine was against my prayer and strivings; besides, his was committed with much deliberation, but mine in a fearful hurry, on a sudden; all this while I was tossed to and fro, like the locusts, and

driven from trouble to sorrow; hearing always the sound of Esau's fall in mine ears, and of the dreadful consequences thereof.

159. Yet this consideration about Judas, his sin, was, for a while, some little relief unto me; for I saw I had not, as to the circumstances, transgressed so foully as he. But this was quickly gone again, for, I thought with myself, there might be more ways than one to commit the unpardonable sin; also I thought that there might be degrees of that, as well as of other transgressions; wherefore, for aught I yet could perceive, this iniquity of mine might be such, as might never be passed by.

160. I was often now ashamed, that I should be like such an ugly man as Judas; I thought, also, how loathsome I should be unto all the saints at the day of judgment; insomuch, that now I could scarce see a good man, that I believed had a good conscience, but I should feel my heart tremble at him, while I was in his presence. Oh! now I saw a glory in walking with God, and what a mercy it was to have a good conscience before him.

161. I was much about this time tempted to content myself, by receiving some false opinion; as that there should be no such thing as a day of judgment, that we should not rise again, and that sin was no such grievous thing; the tempter suggesting thus, For if these things should indeed be true, yet to believe otherwise, would yield you ease for the present. If you must perish, never torment yourself so much beforehand; drive the thoughts of damning out of your mind, by possessing your mind with some such conclusions that Atheists and Ranters do use to help themselves withal.

162. But, oh! when such thoughts have led through my heart, how, as it were, within a step, hath death and judgment been in my view! methought the judge stood at the door, I was as if it was come already; so that such things could have no entertainment. But, methinks, I see by this, that Satan will use any means to keep the soul from Christ; he loveth not an awakened frame of spirit; security, blindness, darkness, and error is the very kingdom and habitation of the wicked one.

163. I found it hard work now to pray to God, because despair was swallowing me up; I thought I was, as with a tempest, driven away from God, for always when I cried to God for mercy, this would come in, It is too late, I am lost, God hath let me fall; not to my correction, but condemnation; my sin is unpardonable; and I know, concerning Esau, how that, after he had sold his birthright, he would have received the blessing, but was rejected. About this time, I did light on that dreadful story of that miserable mortal, Francis Spira; a book that was to my troubled spirit as salt, when rubbed into a fresh wound; every sentence in that book, every groan of that man, with all the rest of his actions in his dolours, as his tears, his prayers, his gnashing of teeth, his wringing of hands, his twining and twisting, languishing and pining away under that mighty hand of God that was upon him, was as knives and daggers in my soul; especially that sentence of his was frightful to me, Man knows the beginning of sin, but who bounds the issues thereof? Then would the former sentence, as the conclusion of all, fall like a hot thunderbolt again upon my conscience; "for you know how that afterward, when he would have inherited the blessing, he was rejected; for he found no place of repentance, though he sought it carefully with tears."

164. Then was I struck into a very great trembling, insomuch that at sometimes I could, for whole days together, feel my very body, as well as my mind, to shake and totter under the sense of the dreadful judgment of God, that should fall on those that have sinned that most fearful and unpardonable sin. I felt also such a clogging and heat at my stomach, by reason of this my terror, that I was, especially at some times, as if my breast bone would have split in sunder; then I thought of that concerning Judas, who, by his falling headlong, burst asunder, and all his bowels gushed out (*Acts i. 18*).

165. I feared also that this was the mark that the Lord did set on Cain, even continual fear and trembling, under the heavy load of guilt that he had charged on him for the blood of his brother Abel. Thus did I wind, and

twine, and shrink, under the burden that was upon me; which burden also did so oppress me, that I could neither stand, nor go, nor lie, either at rest or quiet.

166. Yet that saying would sometimes come to my mind, He hath received gifts for the rebellious (*Ps. lxviii. 18*). "The rebellious," thought I; why, surely they are such as once were under subjection to their prince, even those who, after they have sworn subjection to his government, have taken up arms against him; and this, thought I, is my very condition; once I loved him, feared him, served him; but now I am a rebel; I have sold him, I have said, Let him go if he will; but yet he has gifts for rebels, and then why not for me?

167. This sometimes I thought on, and should labour to take hold thereof, that some, though small, refreshment might have been conceived by me; but in this also I missed of my desire, I was driven with force beyond it, I was like a man that is going to the place of execution, even by that place where he would fain creep in and hide himself, but may not.

168. Again, after I had thus considered the sins of the *saints* in particular, and found mine went beyond them, then I began to think thus with myself: Set the case I should put all theirs together, and mine alone against them, might I not then find some encouragement? For if mine, though bigger than any one, yet should but be equal to all, then there is hopes; for that blood that hath virtue enough in it to wash away all theirs, hath also virtue enough in it to do away mine, though this one be full as big, if no bigger, than all theirs. Here, again, I should consider the sin of David, of Solomon, of Manasseh, of Peter, and the rest of the great offenders; and should also labour, what I might with fairness to aggravate and heighten their sins by several circumstances: but, alas! it was all in vain.

169. I should think with myself that David shed blood to cover his adultery, and that by the sword of the children of Ammon; a work that could not be done but by continuance and deliberate contrivance, which was a great aggravation to his sin. But then this would turn

upon me: Ah! but these were but sins against the law, from which there was a Jesus sent to save them; but yours is a sin against the Saviour, and who shall save you from that?

170. Then I thought on Solomon, and how he sinned in loving strange women, in falling away to their idols, in building them temples, in doing this after light, in his old age, after great mercy received; but the same conclusion that cut me off in the former consideration, cut me off as to this; namely, that all those were but sings against the law, for which God had provided a remedy; but I had sold my Saviour, and there now remained no more sacrifice for sin.

171. I would then add to those men's sins, the sins of Manasseh, how that he built altars for idols in the house of the Lord; he also observed times, used enchantment, had to do with wizards, was a wizard, had his familiar spirits, burned his children in the fire in sacrifice to devils, and made the streets of Jerusalem run down with the blood of innocents. These, thought I, are great sins, sins of a bloody colour; yea, it would turn again upon me: They are none of them of the nature of yours; you have parted with Jesus, you have sold your Saviour.

172. This one consideration would always kill my heart, My sin was point-blank against my Saviour; and that too, at that height, that I had in my heart said of him, Let him go if he will. Oh! methought, this sin was bigger than the sins of a country, of a kingdom, or of the whole world, no one pardonable, nor all of them together, was able to equal mine; mine outwent them every one.

173. Now I should find my mind to flee from God, as from the face of a dreadful judge; yet this was my torment, I could not escape his hand: "It is a fearful thing to fall into the hands of the living God" (*Heb. x. 31*). But blessed be his grace, that scripture, in these flying sins, would call as running after me, "I have blotted out, as a thick cloud, thy transgressions; and, as a cloud, thy sins: return unto me, for I have redeemed thee" (*Is. xliv. 22*). This, I say, would come in upon my

mind, when I was fleeing from the face of God; for I did flee from his face, that is, my mind and spirit fled before him; by reason of his highness, I could not endure; then would the text cry, "Return unto me"; it would cry aloud with a very great voice, "Return unto me, for I have redeemed thee." Indeed, this would make me make a little stop, and, as it were, look over my shoulder behind me, to see if I could discern that the God of grace did follow me with a pardon in his hand, but I could no sooner do that, but all would be clouded and darkened again by that sentence, "For you know how that afterward, when he would have inherited the blessing, he found no place of repentance, though he sought it carefully with tears." Wherefore I could not return, but fled, though at sometimes it cried, "Return, return," as if it did holloa after me. But I feared to close in therewith, lest it should not come from God; for that other, as I said, was still sounding in my conscience, "For you know how that afterward, when he would have inherited the blessing, he was rejected," etc.

174. Once as I was walking to and fro in a good man's shop, bemoaning of myself in my sad and doleful state, afflicting myself with self-abhorrence for this wicked and ungodly thought; lamenting, also, this hard hap of mine, for that I should commit so great a sin, greatly fearing I should not be pardoned; praying, also, in my heart, that if this sin of mine did differ from that against the Holy Ghost, the Lord would show it me. And being now ready to sink with fear, suddenly there was, as if there had rushed in at the window, the noise of wind upon me, but very pleasant, and as if I heard a voice speaking, Didst ever refuse to be justified by the blood of Christ? And, withal my whole life and profession past was, in a moment, opened to me, wherein I was made to see that designedly I had not; so my heart answered groaningly, No. Then fell, with power, that word of God upon me, "See that ye refuse not him that speaketh" (*Heb. xii. 25*). This made a strange seizure upon my spirit; it brought light with it, and commanded a silence in my heart of all those tumultuous thoughts that before did use, like

masterless hell-hounds, to roar and bellow, and make a hideous noise within me. It showed me, also, that Jesus Christ had yet a word of grace and mercy for me, that he had not, as I had feared, quite forsaken and cast off my soul; yea, this was a kind of a chide for my proneness to desperation; a kind of a threatening me if I did not, notwithstanding my sins and the heinousness of them, venture my salvation upon the Son of God. But as to my determining about this strange dispensation, what it was I knew not; or from whence it came I know not. I have not yet, in twenty years' time, been able to make a judgment of it; I thought then what here I shall be loath to speak. But verily, that sudden rushing wind was as if an angel had come upon me; but both it and the salvation I will leave until the day of judgment; only this I say, it commanded a great calm in my soul, it persuaded me there might be hope; it showed me, as I thought, what the sin unpardonable was, and that my soul had yet the blessed privilege to flee to Jesus Christ for mercy. But, I say, concerning this dispensation, I know not what yet to say unto it; which was, also, in truth, the cause that, at first, I did not speak of it in the book; I do now, also, leave it to be thought on by men of sound judgment. I lay not the stress of my salvation thereupon, but upon the Lord Jesus, in the promise; yet, seeing I am here unfolding of my secret things, I thought it might not be altogether inexpedient to let this also show itself, though I cannot now relate the matter as there I did experience it. This lasted, in the savour of it, for about three or four days, and then I began to mistrust and to despair again.

175. Wherefore, still my life hung in doubt before me, not knowing which way I should tip; only this I found my soul desire, even to cast itself at the foot of grace, by prayer and supplication. But, oh! it was hard for me now to bear the face to pray to this Christ for mercy, against whom I had thus most vilely sinned; it was hard work, I say, to offer to look him in the face against whom I had so vilely sinned; and, indeed, I have found it as difficult to come to God by prayer, after backsliding from him, as to

do any other thing. Oh, the shame that did now attend me! especially when I thought I am now a-going to pray to him for mercy that I had so lightly esteemed but a while before! I was ashamed, yea, even confounded, because this villany had been committed by me; but I saw there was but one way with me, I must go to him and humble myself unto him, and beg that he, of his wonderful mercy, would show pity to me, and have mercy upon my wretched sinful soul.

176. Which, when the tempter perceived, he strongly suggested to me, That I ought not to pray to God; for prayer was not for any in my case, neither could it do me good, because I had rejected the Mediator, by whom all prayer came with acceptance to God the Father, and without whom no prayer could come into his presence. Wherefore, now to pray is but to add sin to sin; yea, now to pray, seeing God has cast you off, is the next way to anger and offend him more than you ever did before.

177. For God, saith he, hath been weary of you for these several years already, because you are none of his; your bawlings in his ears hath been no pleasant voice to him; and, therefore, he let you sin this sin, that you might be quite cut off; and will you pray still? This the devil urged, and set forth that, in Numbers, when Moses said to the children of Israel, That because they would not go up to possess the land when God would have them, therefore, for ever after, God did bar them out from thence, though they prayed they might, with tears (*Num. xiv. 36, 37*, etc.).

178. As it is said in another place (*Exod. xxi. 14*), the man that sins presumptuously shall be taken from God's altar, that he may die; even as Joab was by King Solomon, when he thought to find shelter there (*1 Kings ii. 28*, etc.). These places did pinch me very sore; yet, my case being desperate, I thought with myself I can but die; and if it must be so, it shall once be said, that such an one died at the foot of Christ in prayer. This I did, but with great difficulty, God doth know; and that because, together with this, still that saying about Esau would be set at my heart, even like a flaming sword, to keep the

way of the tree of life, lest I should taste thereof and live. Oh! who knows how hard a thing I found it to come to God in prayer.

179. I did also desire the prayers of the people of God for me, but I feared that God would give them no heart to do it; yea, I trembled in my soul to think that some or other of them would shortly tell me, that God had said those words to them that he once did say to the prophet concerning the children of Isreal, "Pray not thou for this people," for I have rejected them (*Jer. xi. 14*). So, pray not for him, for I have rejected him. Yea, I thought that he had whispered this to some of them already, only they durst not tell me so, neither durst I ask them of it, for fear, if it should be so, it would make me quite beside myself. Man knows the beginning of sin, said Spira, but who bounds the issues thereof?

180. About this time I took an opportunity to break my mind to an ancient Christian, and told him all my case; I told him, also, that I was afraid that I had sinned the sin against the Holy Ghost; and he told me he thought so too. Here, therefore, I had but cold comfort; but, talking a little more with him, I found him, though a good man, a stranger to much combat with the devil. Wherefore, I went to God again, as well as I could, for mercy still.

181. Now, also, did the tempter begin to mock me in my misery, saying, that, seeing I had thus parted with the Lord Jesus, and provoked him to displeasure, who would have stood between my soul and the flame of devouring fire, there was now but one way, and that was, to pray that God the Father would be the Mediator betwixt his Son and me, that we might be reconciled again, and that I might have that blessed benefit in him that his blessed saints enjoyed.

182. Then did that scripture seize upon my soul, He is of one mind, and who can turn him? Oh! I saw it was as easy to persuade him to make a new world, a new convenant, or new Bible, besides that we have already, as to pray for such a thing. This was to persuade him that what he had done already was mere folly, and persuade with him to alter, yea, to disannul, the whole

way of salvation; and then would that saying rend my
soul asunder, "Neither is there salvation in any other: for
there is none other name under heaven, given among
men, whereby we must be saved" (*Acts iv. 12*).

183. Now, the most free, and full, and gracious words
of the gospel were the greatest torment to me; yea,
nothing so afflicted me as the thoughts of Jesus Christ,
the remembrance of a Saviour; because I had cast him
off, brought forth the villany of my sin, and my loss by it
to mind; nothing did twinge my conscience like this.
Every time that I thought of the Lord Jesus, of his grace,
love, goodness, kindness, gentleness, meekness, death,
blood, promises and blessed exhortations, comforts and
consolations, it went to my soul like a sword; for still,
unto these my considerations of the Lord Jesus, these
thoughts would make place for themselves in my heart;
aye, this is the Jesus, the loving Saviour, the Son of
God, whom thou hast parted with, whom you slighted,
despised, and abused. This is the only Saviour, the only
Redeemer, the only one that could so love sinners as to
wash them from their sins in his own most precious
blood; but you have no part nor lot in this Jesus, you
have put him from you, you have said in your heart, Let
him go if he will. Now, therefore, you are severed from
him; you have severed yourself from him. Behold, then,
his goodness, but yourself to be no partaker of it. Oh,
thought I, what have I lost! What have I parted with!
What have I disinherited my poor soul of! Oh! it is sad to
be destroyed by the grace and mercy of God; to have the
Lamb, the Saviour, turn lion and destroyer (*Rev. vi.*). I
also trembled, as I have said, at the sight of the saints of
God, especially at those that greatly loved him, and that
made it their business to walk continually with him in
this world; for they did, both in their words, their
carriages, and all their expressions of tenderness and fear
to sin against their precious Saviour, condemn, lay guilt
upon, and also add continual affliction and shame unto
my soul. The dread of them was upon me, and I
trembled at God's Samuels (*1 Sam. xvi. 4*).

184. Now, also, the tempter began afresh to mock my

soul another way, saying that Christ, indeed, did pity my case, and was sorry for my loss; but forasmuch as I had sinned and transgressed, as I had done, he could by no means help me, nor save me from what I feared; for my sin was not of the nature of theirs for whom he bled and died, neither was it counted with those that were laid to his charge when he hanged on the tree. Therefore, unless he should come down from heaven and die anew for this sin, though, indeed, he did greatly pity me, yet I could have no benefit of him. These things may seem ridiculous to others, even as ridiculous as they were in themselves, but to me they were most tormenting cogitations; every of them augmented my misery, that Jesus Christ should have so much love as to pity me when he could not help me; nor did I think that the reason why he could not help me was because his merits were weak, or his grace and salvation spent on them already, but because his faithfulness to his threatening would not let him extend his mercy to me. Besides, I thought, as I have already hinted, that my sin was not within the bounds of that pardon that was wrapped up in a promise; and if not, then I knew assuredly, that it was more easy for heaven and earth to pass away than for me to have eternal life. So that the ground of all these fears of mine did arise from a steadfast belief that I had of the stability of the holy Word of God, and, also, from my being misinformed of the nature of my sin.

185. But, oh! how this would add to my affliction, to conceit that I should be guilty of such a sin for which he did not die. These thoughts would so confound me, and imprison me, and tie me up from faith, that I knew not what to do; but, oh! thought I, that he would come down again! Oh! that the work of man's redemption was yet to be done by Christ! How would I pray him and entreat him to count and reckon this sin amongst the rest for which he died! But this scripture would strike me down as dead, "Christ being raised from the dead dieth no more; death hath no more dominion over him" (*Rom. vi. 9*).

186. Thus, by the strange and unusual assaults of the

tempter, was my soul, like a broken vessel, driven as with the winds, and tossed sometimes headlong into despair, sometimes upon the covenant of works, and sometimes to wish that the new covenant, and the conditions thereof, might, so far forth as I thought myself concerned, be turned another way and changed. But in all these I was but as those that justle against the rocks; more broken, scattered, and rent. Oh, the unthought of imaginations, frights, fears, and terrors that are affected by a thorough application of guilt, yielded to desperation! this is the man that hath "his dwelling among the tombs" with the dead; that is, always crying out and "cutting himself with stones" (*Mark v.* 2–5). But I say, all in vain; desperation will not comfort him, the old covenant will not save him; nay, heaven and earth shall pass away before one jot or tittle of the Word and law of grace shall fall or be removed. This I saw, this I felt, and under this I groaned; yet this advantage I got thereby, namely, a further confirmation of the certainty of the way of salvation, and that the Scriptures were the Word of God! Oh! I cannot now express what then I saw and felt of the steadiness of Jesus Christ, the rock of man's salvation; what was done could not be undone, added to, nor altered I saw, indeed, that sin might drive the soul beyond Christ, even the sin which is unpardonable; but woe to him that was so driven, for the Word would shut him out.

187. Thus was I always sinking, whatever I did think or do. So one day I walked to a neighbouring town, and sat down upon a settle in the street, and fell into a very deep pause about the most fearful state my sin had brought me to; and, after long musing, I lifted up my head, but methought I saw as if the sun that shineth in the heavens did grudge to give light, and as if the very stones in the street, and tiles upon the houses, did bend themselves against me; methought that they all combined together to banish me out of the world; I was abhorred of them, and unfit to dwell among them, or be partaker of their benefits, because I had sinned against the Saviour. O how happy, now, was every creature over

what I was; for they stood fast and kept their station, but I was gone and lost.

188. Then breaking out in the bitterness of my soul, I said to myself, with a grievous sigh, How can God comfort such a wretch as I? I had no sooner said it but this returned upon me, as an echo doth answer a voice, This sin is not unto death. At which I was as if I had been raised out of a grave, and cried out again, Lord, how couldest thou find out such a word as this? for I was filled with admiration at the fitness, and, also, at the unexpectedness of the sentence, the fitness of the Word, the rightness of the timing of it, the power, and sweetness, and light, and glory that came with it, also, was marvellous to me to find. I was now, for the time, out of doubt as to that about which I so much was in doubt before; my fears before were, that my sin was not pardonable, and so that I had no right to pray, to repent, etc., or that if I did, it would be of no advantage or profit to me. But now, thought I, if this sin is not unto death, then it is pardonable; therefore, from this I have encouragement to come to God, by Christ, for mercy, to consider the promise of forgiveness as that which stands with open arms to receive me, as well as others. This, therefore, was a great easement to my mind; to wit, that my sin was pardonable, that it was not the sin unto death (*1 John v. 16, 17*). None but those that know what my trouble, by their own experience, was, can tell what relief came to my soul by this consideration; it was a release to me from my former bounds, and a shelter from my former storm. I seemed now to stand upon the same ground with other sinners, and to have as good right to the Word and prayer as any of them.

189. Now, I say, I was in hopes that my sin was not unpardonable, but that there might be hopes for me to obtain forgiveness. But, oh, how Satan did now lay about him for to bring me down again! But he could by no means do it, neither this day nor the most part of the next, for this sentence stood like a mill-post at my back; yet, towards the evening of the next day, I felt this word begin to leave me and to withdraw its supportation from

me, and so I returned to my old fears again, but with a great deal of grudging and peevishness, for I feared the sorrow of despair; nor could my faith now longer retain this word.

190. But the next day, at evening, being under many fears, I went to seek the Lord; and as I prayed, I cried, and my soul cried to him in these words, with strong cries: O Lord, I beseech thee, show me that thou hast loved me with everlasting love (*Jer. xxxi. 3*). I had no sooner said it but, with sweetness, this returned upon me, as an echo or sounding again, "I have loved thee with an everlasting love." Now I went to bed at quiet; also, when I awaked the next morning, it was fresh upon my soul—and I believed it.

191. But yet the tempter left me not; for it could not be so little as an hundred times that he that day did labour to break my peace. Oh! the combats and conflicts that I did then meet with as I strove to hold by this word; that of Esau would fly in my face like to lightning. I should be sometimes up and down twenty times in an hour, yet God did bear me up and keep my heart upon this word, from which I had also, for several days together, very much sweetness and comfortable hopes of pardon; for thus it was made out to me, I loved thee whilst thou wast committing this sin, I loved thee before, I love thee still, and I will love thee for ever.

192. Yet I saw my sin most barbarous, and a filthy crime, and could not but conclude, and that with great shame and astonishment, that I had horribly abused the holy Son of God; wherefore, I felt my soul greatly to love and pity him, and my bowels to yearn towards him; for I saw he was still my Friend, and did reward me good for evil; yea, the love and affection that then did burn within to my Lord and Saviour Jesus Christ did work, at this time, such a strong and hot desire of revengement upon myself for the abuse I had done unto him, that, to speak as then I thought, had I had a thousand gallons of blood within my veins, I could freely then have spilt it all at the command and feet of this my Lord and Saviour.

193. And as I was thus in musing and in my studies,

considering how to love the Lord and to express my love to him, that saying came in upon me, "If thou, Lord, shouldest mark iniquities, O Lord, who shall stand? But *there is* forgiveness with thee, that thou mayest be feared" (*Ps. cxxx. 3, 4*). These were good words to me, especially the latter part thereof; to wit, that there is forgiveness with the Lord, that he might be feared; that is, as then I understood it, that he might be loved and had in reverence; for it was thus made out to me, that the great God did set so high an esteem upon the love of his poor creatures, that rather than he would go without their love he would pardon their transgressions.

194. And now was that word fulfilled on me, and I was also refreshed by it, Then shall they be ashamed and confounded, "and never open their mouth any more because of their shame, when I am pacified toward them for all that they have done, saith the Lord God" (*Ezek. xvi. 63*). Thus was my soul at this time, and, as I then did think, for ever, set at liberty from being again afflicted with my former guilt and amazement.

195. But before many weeks were over I began to despond again, fearing lest, notwithstanding all that I had enjoyed, that yet I might be deceived and destroyed at the last; for this consideration came strong into my mind, that whatever comfort and peace I thought I might have from the Word of the promise of life, yet unless there could be found in my refreshment a concurrence and agreement in the Scriptures, let me think what I will thereof, and hold it never so fast, I should find no such thing at the end; "for the Scripture cannot be broken" (*John. x. 35*).

196. Now began my heart again to ache and fear I might meet with disappointment at the last; wherefore I began, with all seriousness, to examine my former comfort, and to consider whether one that had sinned as I have done, might with confidence trust upon the faithfulness of God, laid down in those words by which I had been comforted and on which I had leaned myself. But now were brought those sayings to my mind, "For *it is* impossible for those who were once enlightened,

and have tasted of the heavenly gift, and were made partakers of the Holy Ghost, and have tested the good word of God, and the powers of the world to come, if they shall fall away, to renew them again unto repentance" (*Heb. vi. 4–6*). "For if we sin wilfully after that we have received the knowledge of the truth, there remaineth no more sacrifice for sins, but a certain fearful looking for of judgment and fiery indignation, which shall devour the adversaries" (*Heb. x. 26, 27*). Even "as Esau, who for one morsel of meat sold his birthright; for ye know how that afterward, when he would have inherited the blessing, he was rejected; for he found no place of repentance, though he sought it carefully with tears" (*Heb. xii. 16, 17*).

197. Now was the word of the gospel forced from my soul, so that no promise or encouragement was to be found in the Bible for me; and now would that saying work upon my spirit to afflict me, "Rejoice not, O Israel, for joy as *other* people" (*Hos. ix. 1*). For I saw indeed there was cause of rejoicing for those that held to Jesus; but as for me, I had cut myself off by my transgressions, and left myself neither foot-hold, nor hand-hold, amongst all the stays and props in the precious word of life.

198. And truly I did now feel myself to sink into a gulf, as an house whose foundation is destroyed; I did liken myself, in this condition, unto the case of a child that was fallen into a mill-pit, who, though it could make some shift to scrabble and spraul in the water, yet because it could find neither hold for hand nor foot, therefore at last it must die in that condition. So soon as this fresh assault had fastened on my soul, that scripture came into my heart, "That *is* for *many* days" (*Dan. x. 14*). And indeed I found it was so; for I could not be delivered, nor brought to peace again, until well-nigh two years and an half were completely finished. Wherefore these words, though in themselves they tended to discouragement, yet to me, who feared this condition would be eternal, they were at sometimes as an help and refreshment to me.

199. For, thought I, many days are not for ever, many days will have an end, therefore seeing I was to be afflicted, not a few, but many days, yet I was glad it was

but for many days. Thus, I say, I could recal myself sometimes, and give myself a help, for as soon as ever the words came into my mind at first, I knew my trouble would be long; yet this would be but sometimes, for I could not always think on this, nor ever be helped by it, though I did.

200. Now, while these Scriptures lay before me, and laid sin anew at my door, that saying in the eighteenth of Luke, with others, did encourage me to prayer. Then the tempter again laid at me very sore, suggesting, That neither the mercy of God, nor yet the blood of Christ, did at all concern me, nor could they help me for my sin; therefore it was in vain to pray. Yet, thought I, I will pray. But, said the tempter, your sin is unpardonable. Well, said I, I will pray. It is to no boot, said he. Yet, said I, I will pray. So I went to prayer to God; and while I was at prayer, I uttered words to this effect, Lord, Satan tells me that neither thy mercy, nor Christ's blood, is sufficient to save my soul; Lord, shall I honour thee most, by believing thou wilt and canst? or him, by believing thou neither wilt nor canst? Lord, I would fain honour thee, by believing thou wilt and canst.

201. And as I was thus before the Lord, that scripture fastened on my heart, "O woman, great *is* thy faith" (*Matt. xv. 28*), even as if one had clapped me on the back, as I was on my knees before God. Yet I was not able to believe this, that this was a prayer of faith, till almost six months after; for I could not think that I had faith, or that there should be a word for me to act faith on; therefore I should still be as sticking in the jaws of desperation, and went mourning up and down in a sad condition, crying, Is his mercy clean gone? Is his mercy clean gone for ever? And I thought sometimes, even when I was groaning in these expressions, they did seem to make a question whether it was or no; yet I greatly feared it was.

202. There was nothing now that I longed for more than to be put out of doubt, as to this thing in question; and, as I was vehemently desiring to know if there was indeed hopes for me, these words came rolling into my

mind, "Will the Lord cast off for ever? And will he be favourable no more? Is his mercy clean gone for ever? Doth his promise fail for evermore? Hath God forgotten to be gracious? Hath he in anger shut up his tender mercies?" (*Ps. lxxvii.* 7–9). And all the while they run in my mind, methought I had this still as the answer, It is a question whether he had or no; it may be he hath not. Yea, the interrogatory seemed to me to carry in it a sure affirmation that indeed he had not, nor would so cast off, but would be favourable; that his promise doth not fail, and that he had not forgotten to be gracious, nor would in anger shut up his tender mercy. Something, also, there was upon my heart at the same time, which I now cannot call to mind; which, with this text, did sweeten my heart, and made me conclude that his mercy might not be quite gone, nor clean gone for ever.

203. At another time, I remember I was again much under the question, Whether the blood of Christ was sufficient to save my soul? In which doubt I continued from morning till about seven or eight at night; and at last, when I was, as it were, quite worn out with fear, lest it should not lay hold on me, these words did sound suddenly within my heart, He is able. But methought this word ABLE was spoke so loud unto me; it showed such a great word, it seemed to be writ in great letters, and gave such a justle to my fear and doubt, I mean for the time it tarried with me, which was about a day, as I never had from that all my life, either before or after that (*Heb. vii.* 25).

204. But one morning, when I was again at prayer, and trembling under the fear of this, that no word of God could help me, that piece of a sentence darted in upon me, "My grace is sufficient." At this methought I felt some stay, as if there might be hopes. But, oh, how good a thing it is for God to send his Word! For about a fortnight before I was looking on this very place, and then I thought it could not come near my soul with comfort, therefore I threw down my book in a pet. Then I thought it was not large enough for me; no, not large enough; but now, it was as if it had arms of grace so wide

that it could not only enclose me, but many more besides.

205. By these words I was sustained, yet not without exceeding conflicts, for the space of seven or eight weeks; for my peace would be in and out, sometimes twenty times a day; comfort now, and trouble presently; peace now, and before I could go a furlong as full of fear and guilt as ever heart could hold; and this was not only now and then, but my whole seven weeks' experience; for this about the sufficiency of grace, and that of Esau's parting with his birthright, would be like a pair of scales within my mind, sometimes one end would be uppermost, and sometimes again the other; according to which would be my peace or trouble.

206. Therefore I still did pray to God, that he would come in with this scripture more fully on my heart; to wit, that he would help me to apply the whole sentence, for as yet I could not: that he gave, I gathered; but farther I could not go, for as yet it only helped me to hope there might be mercy for me, "My grace is sufficient"; and though it came no farther, it answered my former question; to wit, that there was hope; yet, because "for thee" was left out, I was not contented, but prayed to God for that also. Wherefore, one day as I was in a meeting of God's people, full of sadness and terror, for my fears again were strong upon me; and as I was now thinking my soul was never the better, but my case most sad and fearful, these words did, with great power, suddenly break in upon me, "My grace is sufficient for thee, my grace is sufficient for thee, my grace is sufficient for thee," three times together; and, oh! methought that every word was a mighty word unto me; as *my*, and *grace*, and *sufficient*, and *for thee*; they were then, and sometimes are still, far bigger than others be.

207. At which time my understanding was so enlightened, that I was as though I had seen the Lord Jesus look down from heaven through the tiles upon me, and direct these words unto me. This sent me mourning home, it broke my heart, and filled me full of joy, and laid me low as the dust; only it stayed not long with me,

I mean in this glory and refreshing comfort, yet it continued with me for several weeks, and did encourage me to hope. But so soon as that powerful operation of it was taken off my heart, that other about Esau returned upon me as before; so my soul did hang as in a pair of scales again, sometimes up and sometimes down, now in peace, and anon again in terror.

208. Thus I went on for many weeks, sometimes comforted, and sometimes tormented; and, especially at some times, my torment would be very sore, for all those scriptures forenamed in the Hebrews, would be set before me, as the only sentences that would keep me out of heaven. Then, again, I should begin to repent that ever that thought went through me, I should also think thus with myself, Why, how many scriptures are there against me? There are but three or four: and cannot God miss them, and save me for all them? Sometimes, again, I should think, Oh! if it were not for these three or four words, now how might I be comforted? And I could hardly forbear, at some times, but to wish them out of the book.

209. Then methought I should see as if both Peter, and Paul, and John, and all the writers, did look with scorn upon me, and hold me in derision; and as if they said unto me, All our words are truth, one of as much force as another. It is not we that have cut you off, but you have cast away yourself; there is none of our sentences that you must take hold upon but these, and such as these: "It is impossible; there remains no more sacrifice for sin" (*Heb. vi.*). And "it had been better for them not to have known" the will of God, "than, after they have known *it*, to turn from the holy commandment delivered unto them" (*2 Pet. ii. 21*). "For the Scriptures cannot be broken."

210. These, as the elders of the city of refuge, I saw were to be the judges both of my case and me, while I stood, with the avenger of blood at my heels, trembling at their gate for deliverance, also with a thousand fears and mistrusts, I doubted that they would shut me out for ever (*Josh. xx. 3, 4*).

211. Thus was I confounded, not knowing what to do, nor how to be satisfied in this question, Whether the scriptures could agree in the salvation of my soul? I quaked at the apostles, I knew their words were true, and that they must stand for ever.

212. And I remember one day, as I was in diverse frames of spirit, and considering that these frames were still according to the nature of the several scriptures that came in upon my mind; if this of grace, then was I quiet; but if that of Esau, then tormented; Lord, thought I, if both these scriptures would meet in my heart at once, I wonder which of them would get the better of me. So methought I had a longing mind that they might come both together upon me; yea, I desired of God they might.

213. Well, about two or three days after, so they did indeed; they bolted both upon me at a time, and did work and struggle strangely in me for a while; at last, that about Esau's birthright began to wax weak, and withdraw, and vanish; and this about the sufficiency of grace prevailed with peace and joy. And as I was in a muse about this thing, that scripture came home upon me, "Mercy rejoiceth against judgment" (*Jas. ii. 13*).

214. This was a wonderment to me; yet truly I am apt to think it was of God; for the word of the law and wrath must give place to the word of life and grace; because, though the word of condemnation be glorious, yet the word of life and salvation doth far exceed in glory (*2 Cor. iii. 8–12; Mark ix. 5–7*). Also, that Moses and Elias must both vanish, and leave Christ and his saints alone.

215. This scripture did also most sweetly visit my soul, "And him that cometh to me I will in no wise cast out" (*John vi. 37*). Oh, the comfort that I have had from this word, "in no wise"! as who should say, by no means, for no thing, whatever he hath done. But Satan would greatly labour to pull this promise from me, telling of me that Christ did not mean me, and such as I, but sinners of a lower rank, that had not done as I had done. But I I should answer him again, Satan, here is in this word no such exception; but "him that comes," HIM, any him; "him that cometh to me I will in no wise cast out." And

this I well remember still, that of all the sleights that Satan used to take this scripture from me, yet he never did so much as put this question, But do you come aright? And I have thought the reason was, because he thought I knew full well what coming aright was; for I saw that to come aright was to come as I was, a vile and ungodly sinner, and to cast myself at the feet of mercy, condemning myself for sin. If ever Satan and I did strive for any word of God in all my life, it was for this good word of Christ; he at one end and I at the other. Oh, what work did we make! It was for this in John, I say, that we did so tug and strive; he pulled and I pulled; but, God be praised, I got the better of him, I got some sweetness from it.

216. But, notwithstanding all these helps and blessed words of grace, yet that of Esau's selling of his birthright would still at times distress my conscience; for though I had been most sweetly comforted, and that but just before, yet when that come into my mind, it would make me fear again, I could not be quite rid thereof, it would every day be with me: wherefore now I went another way to work, even to consider the nature of this blasphemous thought; I mean, if I should take the words at the largest, and give them their own natural force and scope, even every word therein. So when I had thus considered, I found, that if they were fairly taken, they would amount to this, that I had freely left the Lord Jesus Christ to his choice, whether he would be my Saviour or no; for the wicked words were these, Let him go if he will. Then that scripture gave me hope, "I will never leave thee nor forsake thee" (*Heb. xiii.* 5). O Lord, said I, but I have left thee. Then it answered again, "But I will not leave thee." For this I thank God also.

217. Yet I was grievously afraid he should, and found it exceeding hard to trust him, seeing I had so offended him. I could have been exceeding glad that this thought had never befallen, for then I thought I could, with more ease and freedom abundance, have leaned upon his grace. I see it was with me, as it was with Joseph's brethren; the guilt of their own wickedness did often fill

them with fears that their brother would at last despise
them (*Gen. l. 15–17*).

218. But above all the scriptures that I yet did meet
with, that in the twentieth of Joshua was the greatest
comfort to me, which speaks of the slayer that was to flee
for refuge. And if the avenger of blood pursue the slayer,
then, saith Moses, they that are the elders of the city of
refuge shall not deliver him into his hand, because he
smote his neighbour unwittingly, and hated him not
aforetime. Oh, blessed be God for this word; I was
convinced that I was the slayer; and that the avenger of
blood pursued me, that I felt with great terror; only now
it remained that I inquire whether I have right to enter
the city of refuge. So I found that he must not, who lay in
wait to shed blood: it was not the wilful murderer, but he
who unwittingly did it, he who did unawares shed blood;
not of spite, or grudge, or malice, he that shed it
unwittingly, even he who did not hate his neighbour
before. Wherefore,

219. I thought verily I was the man that must enter,
because I had smitten my neighbour unwittingly, and
hated him not aforetime. I hated him not aforetime; no, I
prayed unto him, was tender of sinning against him; yea,
and against this wicked temptation I had strove for a
twelvemonth before; yea, and also when it did pass
through my heart, it did in spite of my teeth: wherefore I
thought I had right to enter this city, and the elders,
which are the apostles, were not to deliver me up. This,
therefore, was great comfort to me; and did give me
much ground of hope.

220. Yet being very critical, for my smart had made me
that I knew not what ground was sure enough to bear
me, I had one question that my soul did much desire to
be resolved about; and that was, Whether it be possible
for any soul that hath indeed sinned the unpardonable
sin, yet after that to receive though but the least true
spiritual comfort from God through Christ? The which,
after I had much considered, I found the answer was,
No, they could not; and that for these reasons:

221. First, Because those that have sinned that sin,

they are debarred a share in the blood of Christ, and being shut out of that, they must needs be void of the least ground of hope, and so of spiritual comfort; for to such "there remaineth no more sacrifice for sins" (*Heb. x. 26*). Secondly, Because they are denied a share in the promise of life; they shall never be forgiven, "neither in this world, neither in that which is to come" (*Matt. xii. 32*). Thirdly, The Son of God excludes them also from a share in his blessed intercession, being for ever ashamed to own them both before his holy Father, and the blessed angels in heaven (*Mark viii. 38*).

222. When I had, with much deliberation, considered of this matter, and could not but conclude that the Lord had comforted me, and that too after this my wicked sin; then, methought, I durst venture to come nigh unto those most fearful and terrible scriptures, with which all this while I had been so greatly affrighted, and on which, indeed, before I durst scarce cast mine eye, yea, had much ado an hundred times to forbear wishing of them out of the Bible; for I thought they would destroy me; but now, I say, I began to take some measure of encouragement to come close to them, to read them, and consider them, and to weigh their scope and tendency.

223. The which, when I began to do, I found their visage changed; for they looked not so grimly on me as before I thought they did. And, first, I came to the sixth of the Hebrews, yet trembling for fear it should strike me; which when I had considered, I found that the falling there intended was a falling quite away; that is, as I conceived, a falling from, and an absolute denial of the gospel of remission of sins by Christ; for from them the apostle begins his argument (*ver. 1–3*). Secondly, I found that this falling away must be openly, even in the view of the world, even so as "to put Christ to an open shame." Thirdly, I found that those he there intended were for ever shut up of God, both in blindness, hardness, and impenitency: it is impossible they should be renewed again unto repentance. By all these particulars, I found, to God's everlasting praise, my sin was not the sin in this place intended.

First, I confessed I was fallen, but not fallen away, that is, from the profession of faith in Jesus unto eternal life. Secondly, I confessed that I had put Jesus Christ to shame by my sin, but not to open shame; I did not deny him before men, nor condemn him as a fruitless one before the world. Thirdly, Nor did I find that God had shut me up, or denied me to come, though I found it hard work indeed to come to him by sorrow and repentance. Blessed be God for unsearchable grace.

224. Then I considered that in the tenth of the Hebrews, and found that the wilful sin there mentioned is not every wilful sin, but that which doth throw off Christ, and then his commandments too. Secondly, That must also be done openly, before two or three witnesses, to answer that of the law (*ver. 28*). Thirdly, This sin cannot be committed, but with great despite done to the Spirit of grace; despising both the dissuasions from that sin, and the persuasions to the contrary. But the Lord knows, though this my sin was devilish, yet it did not amount to these.

225. And as touching that in the twelfth of the Hebrews, about Esau's selling his birthright, though this was that which killed me, and stood like a spear against me; yet now I did consider, First, That his was not a hasty thought against the continual labour of his mind, but a thought consented to and put in practice likewise, and that too after some deliberation (*Gen. xxv.*). Secondly, It was a public and open action, even before his brother, if not before many more; this made his sin of a far more heinous nature than otherwise it would have been. Thirdly, He continued to slight his birthright: "He did eat and drink, and went his way; thus Esau despised *his* birthright" (*ver. 34*). Yea, twenty years after, he was found to despise it still. "And Esau said, I have enough, my brother; keep that thou hast unto thyself" (*Gen. xxxiii. 9*).

226. Now as touching this, that Esau sought a place of repentance; thus I thought, first, This was not for the birthright, but for the blessing; this is clear from the apostle, and is distinguished by Esau himself; "he took

away my birthright (that is, formerly); and, behold, now he hath taken away my blessing" (*Gen. xxvii. 36*). Secondly, Now, this being thus considered, I came again to the apostle, to see what might be the mind of God, in a New Testament style and sense, concerning Esau's sin; and so far as I could conceive, this was the mind of God, That the birthright signified regeneration, and the blessing the eternal inheritance; for so the apostle seems to hint, "Lest there *be* any profane person, as Esau, who for one morsel of meat sold his birthright"; as if he should say, Lest there be any person amongst you that shall cast off all those blessed beginnings of God that at present are upon him, in order to a new birth, lest they become as Esau, even be rejected afterwards, when they would inherit the blessing.

227. For many there are who, in the day of grace and mercy, despise those things which are indeed the birthright to heaven, who yet, when the deciding day appears, will cry as loud as Esau, "Lord, Lord, open to us"; but then, as Isaac would not repent, no more will God the Father, but will say, I have blessed these, yea, and they shall be blessed; but as for you, depart from me, all ye workers of iniquity (*Gen. xxvii. 33; Luke xiii. 25–7*).

228. When I had thus considered these scriptures, and found that thus to understand them was not against, but according to other scriptures; this still added further to my encouragement and comfort, and also gave a great blow to that objection, to wit, that the scripture could not agree in the salvation of my soul. And now remained only the hinder part of the tempest, for the thunder was gone beyond me, only some drops did still remain, that now and then would fall upon me; but because my former frights and anguish were very sore and deep, therefore it did oft befal me still, as it befalleth those that have been scared with fire, I thought every voice was Fire, fire; every little touch would hurt my tender conscience.

229. But one day, as I was passing in the field, and that too with some dashes on my conscience, fearing lest yet all was not right, suddenly this sentence fell upon my

soul, Thy righteousness is in heaven; and methought withal, I saw, with the eyes of my soul, Jesus Christ at God's right hand; there, I say, is my righteousness; so that wherever I was, or whatever I was a-doing, God could not say of me, He wants my righteousness, for that was just before him. I also saw, moreover, that it was not my good frame of heart that made my righteousness better, nor yet my bad frame that made my righteousness worse; for my righteousness was Jesus Christ himself, the same yesterday, and to-day, and for ever (*Heb. xiii. 8*).

230. Now did my chains fall off my legs indeed, I was loosed from my affliction and irons, my temptations also fled away; so that, from that time, those dreadful scriptures of God left off to trouble me; now went I also home rejoicing, for the grace and love of God. So when I came home, I looked to see if I could find that sentence, Thy righteousness is in heaven; but could not find such a saying, wherefore my heart began to sink again, only that was brought to my remembrance, he "of God is made unto us wisdom, and righteousness, and sanctification, and redemption"; by this word I saw the other sentence true (*1 Cor. i. 30*).

231. For by this scripture, I saw that the man Christ Jesus, as he is distinct from us, as touching his bodily presence, so he is our righteousness and sanctification before God. Here, therefore, I lived for some time, very sweetly at peace with God through Christ; Oh, methought, Christ! Christ! there was nothing but Christ that was before my eyes, I was not now only for looking upon this and the other benefits of Christ apart, as of his blood, burial, or resurrection, but considered him as a whole Christ! As he in whom all these, and all other his virtues, relations, offices, and operations met together, and that as he sat on the right hand of God in heaven.

232. It was glorious to me to see his exaltation, and the worth and prevalency of all his benefits, and that because of this: now I could look from myself to him, and should reckon that all those graces of God that now were green in me, were yet but like those cracked groats and fourpence-halfpennies that rich men carry in their

purses, when their gold is in their trunks at home! Oh, I
saw my gold was in my trunk at home! In Christ, my
Lord and Saviour! Now Christ was all; all my wisdom,
all my righteousness, all my sanctification, and all my
redemption.

233. Further, the Lord did also lead me into the
mystery of union with the Son of God, that I was joined
to him, that I was flesh of his flesh, and bone of his bone,
and now was that a sweet word to me in *Eph. v. 30*. By
this also was my faith in him, as my righteousness, the
more confirmed to me; for if he and I were one, then his
righteousness was mine, his merits mine, his victory also
mine. Now could I see myself in heaven and earth at
once; in heaven by my Christ, by my head, by my
righteousness and life, though on earth by my body or
person.

234. Now I saw Christ Jesus was looked on of God,
and should also be looked upon by us, as that common or
public person, in whom all the whole body of his elect are
always to be considered and reckoned; that we fulfilled
the law by him, rose from the dead by him, got the
victory over sin, death, the devil, and hell, by him; when
he died, we died; and so of his resurrection. "Thy dead
men shall live, *together with* my dead body shall they
arise," saith he (*Is. xxvi. 19*). And again, "After two days
will he revive us: in the third day he will raise us up, and
we shall live in his sight" (*Hos. vi. 2*); which is now
fulfilled by the sitting down of the Son of man on the
right hand of the Majesty in the heavens, according to
that to the Ephesians, he "hath raised *us* up together, and
made *us* sit together in heavenly *places* in Christ Jesus"
(*Eph. ii. 6*).

235. Ah, these blessed considerations and scriptures,
with many other of a like nature, were in those days
made to spangle in mine eyes, so that I have cause to say,
"Praise ye the Lord. Praise God in his sanctuary: praise
him in the firmament of his power. Praise him for his
mighty acts: praise him according to his excellent
greatness" (*Ps. cl. 1, 2*).

236. Having thus, in few words, given you a taste of the

sorrow and affliction that my soul went under, by the
guilt and terror that this my wicked thought did lay
me under; and having given you also a touch of my
deliverance therefrom, and of the sweet and blessed
comfort that I met with afterwards, which comfort dwelt
about a twelvemonth with my heart, to my unspeakable
admiration; I will now, God willing, before I proceed any
farther, give you in a word or two, what, as I conceive,
was the cause of this temptation; and also after that,
what advantage, at the last, it became unto my soul.

237. For the causes, I conceived they were principally
two: of which two also I was deeply convinced all the
time this trouble lay upon me. The first was, for that I
did not, when I was delivered from the temptation that
went before, still pray to God to keep me from temptations that were to come; for though, as I can say in truth,
my soul was much in prayer before this trial seized me,
yet then I prayed only, or at the most, principally for the
removal of present troubles, and for fresh discoveries of
his love in Christ, which I saw afterwards was not
enough to do; I also should have prayed that the great
God would keep me from the evil that was to come.

238. Of this I was made deeply sensible by the prayer
of holy David, who, when he was under present mercy,
yet prayed that God would hold him back from sin and
temptation to come; "Then," saith he, "shall I be
upright, I shall be innocent from the GREAT transgression" (*Ps. xix. 13*). By this very word was I galled and
condemned, quite through this long temptation.

239. That also was another word that did much
condemn me for my folly, in the neglect of this duty (*Heb.
iv. 16*), "Let us therefore come boldly unto the throne of
grace, that we may obtain mercy, and find grace to help
in time of need." This I had not done, and therefore was
suffered thus to sin and fall, according to what is written,
"Pray that ye enter not into temptation." And truly this
very thing is to this day of such weight and awe upon me,
that I dare not, when I come before the Lord, go off my
knees, until I entreat him for help and mercy against the
temptations that are to come; and I do beseech thee,

reader, that thou learn to beware of my negligence, by the affliction that for this thing I did for days, and months, and years, with sorrow undergo.

240. Another cause of this temptation was, that I had tempted God; and on this manner did I do it. Upon a time my wife was great with child, and before her full time was come, her pangs, as of a woman in travail, were fierce and strong upon her, even as if she would have immediately fallen in labour, and been delivered of an untimely birth. Now, at this very time it was that I had been so strongly tempted to question the being of God; wherefore, as my wife lay crying by me, I said, but with all secrecy imaginable, even thinking in my heart, Lord, if thou wilt now remove this sad affliction from my wife, and cause that she be troubled no more therewith this night, and now were her pangs just upon her, then I shall know that thou canst discern the most secret thoughts of the heart.

241. I had no sooner said it in my heart, but her pangs were taken from her, and she was cast into a deep sleep, and so she continued till morning; at this I greatly marvelled, not knowing what to think; but after I had been awake a good while, and heard her cry no more, I fell to sleeping also. So when I waked in the morning, it came upon me again, even what I had said in my heart the last night, and how the Lord had showed me that he knew my secret thoughts, which was a great astonishment unto me for several weeks after.

242. Well, about a year and a half afterwards, that wicked sinful thought, of which I have spoken before, went through my wicked heart, even this thought, Let Christ go if he will; so when I was fallen under guilt for this, the remembrance of my other thought, and of the effect thereof, would also come upon me with this retort, which also carried rebuke along with it, Now you may see that God doth know the most secret thoughts of the heart.

243. And with this, that of the passages that were betwixt the Lord and his servant Gideon fell upon my spirit; how because that Gideon tempted God with his

fleece, both wet and dry, when he should have believed and ventured upon his word, therefore the Lord did afterwards so try him, as to send him against an innumerable company of enemies; and that too, as to outward appearance, without any strength or help (*Judges vi., vii.*). Thus he served me, and that justly, for I should have believed his word, and not have put an IF upon the all-seeingness of God.

244. And now to show you something of the advantages that I also gained by this temptation; and first, By this I was made continually to possess in my soul a very wonderful sense both of the being and glory of God, and of his beloved Son; in the temptation that went before, my soul was perplexed with unbelief, blasphemy, hardness of heart, questions about the being of God, Christ, the truth of the Word, and certainty of the world to come; I say, then I was greatly assaulted and tormented with atheism; but now the case was otherwise, now was God and Christ continually before my face, though not in a way of comfort, but in a way of exceeding dread and terror. The glory of the holiness of God did at this time break me to pieces; and the bowels and compassion of Christ did break me as on the wheel; for I could not consider him but as a lost and rejected Christ, the remembrance of which was as the continual breaking of my bones.

245. The Scriptures now also were wonderful things unto me; I saw that the truth and verity of them were the keys of the kingdom of heaven; those that the Scriptures favour they must inherit bliss, but those that they oppose and condemn must perish evermore. Oh! this word, "For the Scripture cannot be broken," would rend the caul of my heart; and so would that other, "Whose soever sins ye remit, they are remitted unto them; *and* whose soever *sins* ye retain, they are retained." Now I saw the apostles to be the elders of the city of refuge (*Josh. xx. 4*), those that they were to receive in, were received to life; but those that they shut out were to be slain by the avenger of blood.

246. Oh! one sentence of the Scriptures did more afflict

and terrify my mind, I mean those sentences that stood against me, as sometimes I thought they every one did, more I say, than an army of forty thousand men that might have come against me. Woe be to him against whom the Scriptures bend themselves.

247. By this temptation I was made to see more into the nature of the promises than ever I was before; for I lying now trembling under the mighty hand of God, continually torn and rent by the thunderings of his justice; this made me, with careful heart and watchful eye, with great seriousness, to turn over every leaf, and with much diligence, mixed with trembling, to consider every sentence, together with its natural force and latitude.

248. By this temptation, also, I was greatly beaten off my former foolish practice, of putting by the word of promise when it came into my mind; for now, though I could not suck that comfort and sweetness from the promise as I had done at other times, yea, like to a man a-sinking, I should catch at all I saw; formerly I thought I might not meddle with the promise unless I felt its comfort, but now it was no time thus to do, the avenger of blood too hardly did pursue me.

249. Now therefore I was glad to catch at that word, which yet I feared I had no ground or right to own; and even to leap into the bosom of that promise, that yet I feared did shut its heart against me. Now also I should labour to take the Word as God had laid it down, without restraining the natural force of one syllable thereof. O what did I now see in that blessed sixth of John, "And him that cometh to me I will in no wise cast out" (*ver. 37*). Now I began to consider with myself, that God had a bigger mouth to speak with than I had heart to conceive with. I thought also with myself that he spake not his words in haste, or in unadvised heat, but with infinite wisdom and judgment, and in very truth and faithfulness (*2 Sam. iii. 18*).

250. I should in these days, often in my greatest agonies, even flounce towards the promise, as the horses do towards sound ground that yet stick in the mire,

concluding, though as one almost bereft of his wits through fear, on this I will rest and stay, and leave the fulfilling of it to the God of heaven that made it. Oh! many a pull hath my heart had with Satan for that blessed sixth of John. I did not now, as at other times, look principally for comfort, though, O how welcome would it have been unto me! But now a word, a word to lean a weary soul upon, that I might not sink for ever! it was that I hunted for.

251. Yea, often when I have been making to the promise, I have seen as if the Lord would refuse my soul for ever. I was often as if I had run upon the pikes, and as if the Lord had thrust at me to keep me from him as with a flaming sword. Then I should think of Esther, who went to petition the king contrary to the law (*Es. iv. 16*). I thought also of Benhadad's servants, who went with ropes upon their heads to their enemies for mercy (*1 Kings xx. 31*). The woman of Canaan also, that would not be daunted, though called dog by Christ (*Matt. xv. 20–8*); and the men that went to borrow bread at midnight (*Luke xi. 5–8*), were great encouragements unto me.

252. I never saw those heights and depths in grace, and love, and mercy, as I saw after this temptation. Great sins do draw out great grace; and where guilt is most terrible and fierce there the mercy of God in Christ, when showed to the soul, appears most high and mighty. When Job had passed through his captivity, he had "twice as much as he had before" (*Job xlii. 10*). Blessed be God for Jesus Christ our Lord. Many other things I might here make observation of, but I would be brief, and therefore shall at this time omit them, and do pray God that my harms may make others fear to offend, lest they also be made to bear the iron yoke as I did.

I had two or three times, at or about my deliverance from this temptation, such strange apprehensions of the grace of God, that I could hardly bear up under it, it was so out of measure amazing, when I thought it could reach me, that I do think, if that sense of it had abode long upon me, it would have made me incapable for business.

253. Now I shall go forward to give you a relation of other of the Lord's dealing with me, of his dealings with me at sundry other seasons, and of the temptations I then did meet withal. I shall begin with what I met with when I first did join in fellowship with the people of God in Bedford. After I had propounded to the church that my desire was to walk in the order and ordinances of Christ with them, and was also admitted by them; while I thought of that blessed ordinance of Christ, which was his last supper with his disciples before his death, that scripture, "This do in remembrance of me" (*Luke xxii. 19*), was made a very precious word unto me; for by it the Lord did come down upon my conscience with the discovery of his death for my sins; and as I then felt, did as if he plunged me in the virtue of the same. But, behold, I had not been long a partaker at that ordinance, but such fierce and sad temptations did attend me at all times therein, both to blaspheme the ordinance, and to wish some deadly thing to those that then did eat thereof; that, lest I should at any time be guilty of consenting to these wicked and fearful thoughts, I was forced to bend myself all the while to pray to God to keep me from such blasphemies; and also to cry to God to bless the bread and cup to them as it went from mouth to mouth. The reason of this temptation I have thought since was, because I did not, with that reverence as became me, at first approach to partake thereof.

254. Thus I continued for three-quarters of a year, and could never have rest nor ease; but at last the Lord came in upon my soul with that same scripture by which my soul was visited before; and after that I have been usually very well and comfortable in the partaking of that blessed ordinance, and have, I trust, therein discerned the Lord's body as broken for my sins, and that his precious blood hath been shed for my transgressions.

255. Upon a time I was somewhat inclining to a consumption, wherewith, about the spring, I was suddenly and violently seized with much weakness in my outward man, insomuch that I thought I could not live. Now began I afresh to give myself up to a serious

examination after my state and condition for the future, and of my evidences for that blessed world to come; for it hath, I bless the name of God, been my usual course, as always, so especially in the day of affliction, to endeavour to keep my interest in the life to come clear before my eye.

256. But I had no sooner began to recal to mind my former experience of the goodness of God to my soul, but there came flocking into my mind an innumerable company of my sins and transgressions, amongst which these were at this time most to my affliction, namely, my deadness, dulness, and coldness in holy duties; my wanderings of heart, of my wearisomeness in all good things, my want of love to God, his ways, and people, with this at the end of all, Are these the fruits of Christianity? are these the tokens of a blessed man?

257. At the apprehension of these things my sickness was doubled upon me, for now was I sick in my inward man, my soul was clogged with guilt; now also was my former experience of God's goodness to me quite taken out of my mind, and hid as if it had never been, nor seen. Now was my soul greatly pinched between these two considerations, Live I must not, Die I dare not; now I sunk and fell in my spirit, and was giving up all for lost; but as I was walking up and down in the house, as a man in a most woful state, that word of God took hold of my heart, Ye are "justified freely by his grace, through the redemption that is in Christ Jesus" (*Rom. iii. 24*). But oh, what a turn it made upon me!

258. Now was I as one awakened out of some troublesome sleep and dream, and listening to this heavenly sentence, I was as if I had heard it thus expounded to me: Sinner, thou thinkest that because of thy sins and infirmities I cannot save thy soul, but behold my Son is by me, and upon him I look, and not on thee, and will deal with thee according as I am pleased with him. At this I was greatly lightened in my mind, and made to understand that God could justify a sinner at any time; it was but his looking upon Christ, and imputing of his benefits to us, and the work was forthwith done.

259. And as I was thus in a muse, that scripture also came with great power upon my spirit, "Not by works of righteousness which we have done, but according to his mercy he saved us," etc. (*Tit. iii. 5; 2 Tim. i. 9*). Now was I got on high; I saw myself within the arms of grace and mercy; and though I was before afraid to think of a dying hour, yet now I cried, Let me die. Now death was lovely and beautiful in my sight; for I saw we shall never live indeed till we be gone to the other world. Oh, methought this life is but a slumber in comparison of that above; at this time also I saw more in those words, "Heirs of God" (*Rom. viii. 17*), than ever I shall be able to express while I live in this world. "Heirs of God"! God himself is the portion of the saints. This I saw and wondered at, but cannot tell you what I saw.

260. Again, as I was at another time very ill and weak, all that time also the tempter did beset me strongly, for I find he is much for assaulting the soul when it begins to approach towards the grave, then is his opportunity, labouring to hide from me my former experience of God's goodness; also setting before me the terrors of death and the judgment of God, insomuch that at this time, through my fear of miscarrying for ever, should I now die, I was as one dead before death came, and was as if I had felt myself already descending into the pit; methought, I said, there was no way, but to hell I must; but behold, just as I was in the midst of those fears, these words of the angels carrying Lazarus into Abraham's bosom darted in upon me, as who should say, So it shall be with thee when thou dost leave this world. This did sweetly revive my spirit, and help me to hope in God; which, when I had with comfort mused on a while, that word fell with great weight upon my mind, "O death, where *is* thy sting? O grave, where *is* thy victory?" (*1 Cor. xv. 55*). At this I became both well in body and mind at once, for my sickness did presently vanish, and I walked comfortably in my work for God again.

261. At another time, though just before I was pretty well and savoury in my spirit, yet suddenly there fell upon me a great cloud of darkness, which did so hide

from me the things of God and Christ, that I was as if I had never seen or known them in my life; I was also so overrun in my soul, with a senseless, heartless frame of spirit, that I could not feel my soul to move or stir after grace and life by Christ; I was as if my loins were broken, or as if my hands and feet had been tied or bound with chains. At this time also I felt some weakness to seize upon my outward man, which made still the other affliction the more heavy and uncomfortable to me.

262. After I had been in this condition some three or four days, as I was sitting by the fire, I suddenly felt this word to sound in my heart, I must go to Jesus; at this my former darkness and atheism fled away, and the blessed things of heaven were set within my view. While I was on this sudden thus overtaken with surprise, Wife, said I, is there ever such a scripture, I must go to Jesus? She said she could not tell, therefore I sat musing still to see if I could remember such a place; I had not sat above two or three minutes but that came bolting in upon me, "And to an innumerable company of angels," and withal, Hebrews the twelfth, about the mount Sion, was set before mine eyes (*ver.* 22–4).

263. Then with joy I told my wife, O now I know, I know! But that night was a good night to me, I never had but few better; I longed for the company of some of God's people that I might have imparted unto them what God had showed me. Christ was a precious Christ to my soul that night; I could scarce lie in my bed for joy, and peace, and triumph, through Christ; this great glory did not continue upon me until morning, yet that twelfth of the author to the Hebrews (*ver.* 22–4) was a blessed scripture to me for many days together after this.

264. The words are these, "Ye are come unto mount Sion, and unto the city of the living God, the heavenly Jerusalem, and to an innumerable company of angels, to the general assembly and church of the firstborn, which are written in heaven, and to God the Judge of all, and to the spirits of just men made perfect, and to Jesus the mediator of the new covenant, and to the blood of sprinkling, that speaketh better things than *that of* Abel."

Through this blessed sentence the Lord led me over and over, first to this word, and then to that, and showed me wonderful glory in every one of them. These words also have oft since this time been great refreshment to my spirit. Blessed be God for having mercy on me.

A BRIEF ACCOUNT OF THE AUTHOR'S CALL TO THE WORK OF THE MINISTRY

265. And now I am speaking my experience, I will in this place thrust in a word or two concerning my preaching the Word, and of God's dealing with me in that particular also. For after I had been about five or six years awakened, and helped myself to see both the want and worth of Jesus Christ our Lord, and also enabled to venture my soul upon him, some of the most able among the saints with us, I say the most able for judgment and holiness of life, as they conceived, did perceive that God had counted me worthy to understand something of his will in his holy and blessed Word, and had given me utterance, in some measure, to express what I saw to others for edification; therefore they desired me, and that with much earnestness, that I would be willing, at sometimes, to take in hand, in one of the meetings, to speak a word of exhortation unto them.

266. The which, though at the first it did much dash and abash my spirit, yet being still by them desired and intreated, I consented to their request, and did twice at two several assemblies, but in private, though with much weakness and infirmity, discover my gift amongst them; at which they not only seemed to be, but did solemnly protest, as in the sight of the great God, they were both affected and comforted, and gave thanks to the Father of mercies for the grace bestowed on me.

267. After this, sometimes when some of them did go into the country to teach, they would also that I should go with them; where, though as yet I did not, nor durst not, make use of my gift in an open way, yet more privately still as I came amongst the good people in those

places, I did sometimes speak a word of admonition unto them also; the which, they as the other received, with with rejoicing, at the mercy of God to me-ward, professing their souls were edified thereby.

268. Wherefore, to be brief, at last, being still desired by the church, after some solemn prayer to the Lord, with fasting, I was more particularly called forth, and appointed to a more ordinary and public preaching the word, not only to, and amongst them that believed, but also to offer the gospel to those who had not yet received the faith thereof; about which time I did evidently find in my mind a secret pricking forward thereto; though I bless God, not for desire of vain glory, for at that time I was most sorely afflicted with the fiery darts of the devil concerning my eternal state.

269. But yet could not be content, unless I was found in the exercise of my gift, unto which also I was greatly animated, not only by the continual desires of the godly, but also by that saying of Paul to the Corinthians, "I beseech you, brethren, (ye know the household of Stephanas, that it is the firstfruits of Achaia, and *that* they have addicted themselves to the ministry of the saints,) that ye submit yourselves unto such, and to every one that helpeth with *us*, and laboureth" (*1 Cor. xvi. 15, 16*).

270. By this text I was made to see that the Holy Ghost never intended that men who have gift and abilities should bury them in the earth, but rather did command and stir up such to the exercise of their gift, and also did commend those that were apt and ready so to do, "They have addicted themselves to the ministry of the saints." This scripture, in these days, did continually run in my mind, to encourage me and strengthen me in this my work for God; I have also been encouraged from several other scriptures and examples of the godly, both specified in the Word and other ancient histories (*Acts viii. 4; xviii. 24, 25; 1 Pet. iv. 10; Rom. xii. 6;* Foxe's *Acts and Monuments*).

271. Wherefore, though of myself, of all the saints the most unworthy, yet I, but with great fear and trembling

at the sight of my own weakness, did set upon the work, and did according to my gift, and the proportion of my faith, preach that blessed gospel that God had showed me in the holy Word of truth; which, when the country understood, they came in to hear the Word by hundreds, and that from all parts, though upon sundry and divers accounts.

272. And I thank God he gave unto me some measure of bowels and pity for their souls, which also did put me forward to labour with great diligence and earnestness, to find out such a word as might, if God would bless it, lay hold of and awaken the conscience, in which also the good Lord had respect to the desire of his servant; for I had not preached long before some began to be touched by the Word, and to be greatly afflicted in their minds at the apprehension of the greatness of their sin, and of their need of Jesus Christ.

273. But I at first could not believe that God should speak by me to the heart of any man, still counting myself unworthy; yet those who thus were touched would love me and have a peculiar respect for me; and though I did put it from me, that they should be awakened by me, still they would confess it, and affirm it before the saints of God; they would also bless God for me, unworthy wretch that I am! and count me God's instrument that showed to them the way of salvation.

274. Wherefore, seeing them in both their words and deeds to be so constant, and also in their hearts so earnestly pressing after the knowledge of Jesus Christ, rejoicing that ever God did send me where they were; then I began to conclude it might be so, that God had owned in his work such a foolish one as I, and then came that word of God to my heart with much sweet refreshment, "The blessing of him that was ready to perish came upon me; and I caused the widow's heart to sing for joy" (*Job. xxix. 13*).

275. At this therefore I rejoiced, yea, the tears of those whom God did awaken by my preaching would be both solace and encouragement to me; for I thought on those sayings, "Who is he that maketh me glad but the same

which is made sorry by me?" (*2 Corr. ii. 2*); and again, Though "I be not an apostle to others, yet, doubtless, I am to you: for the seal of mine apostleship are ye in the Lord" (*1 Cor. ix. 2*). These things, therefore, were as another argument unto me that God had called me to, and stood by me in this work.

276. In my preaching of the Word, I took special notice of this one thing, namely, that the Lord did lead me to begin where his Word begins with sinners; that is, to condemn all flesh, and to open and allege that the curse of God, by the law, doth belong to and lay hold on all men as they come into the world, because of sin. Now this part of my work I fulfilled with great sense; for the terrors of the law, and guilt for my transgressions, lay heavy on my conscience. I preached what I felt, what I smartingly did feel, even that under which my poor soul did groan and tremble to astonishment.

277. Indeed I have been as one sent to them from the dead; I went myself in chains to preach to them in chains; and carried that fire in my own conscience that I persuaded them to beware of. I can truly say, and that without dissembling, that when I have been to preach, I have gone full of guilt and terror even to the pulpit door, and there it hath been taken off, and I have been at liberty in my mind until I have done my work, and then immediately, even before I could get down the pulpit stairs, I have been as bad as I was before; yet God carried me on, but surely with a strong hand, for neither guilt nor hell could take me off my work.

278. Thus I went for the space of two years, crying out against men's sins, and their fearful state because of them. After which the Lord came in upon my own soul with some staid peace and comfort through Christ; for he did give me many sweet discoveries of his blessed grace through him. Wherefore now I altered in my preaching, for still I preached what I saw and felt; now therefore I did much labour to hold forth Jesus Christ in all his offices, relations, and benefits unto the world; and did strive also to discover, to condemn, and remove those false supports and props on which the world doth both

lean, and by them fall and perish. On these things also I staid as long as on the other.

279. After this, God led me into something of the mystery of union with Christ; wherefore that I discovered and showed to them also. And when I had travelled through these three chief points of the Word of God, about the space of five years or more, I was caught in my present practice and cast into prison, where I have laid above as long again, to confirm the truth by way of suffering, as I was before in testifying of it according to the Scriptures in a way of preaching.

280. When I have been preaching, I thank God, my heart hath often all the time of this and the other exercise, with great earnestness, cried to God that he would make the Word effectual to the salvation of the soul; still being grieved lest the enemy should take the Word away from the conscience, and so it should become unfruitful. Wherefore I did labour so to speak the Word, as that thereby, if it were possible, the sin and person guilty might be particularised by it.

281. Also, when I have done the exercise, it hath gone to my heart to think the Word should now fall as rain on stony places, still wishing from my heart, O that they who have heard me speak this day did but see as I do what sin, death, hell, and the curse of God is; and also what the grace, and love, and mercy of God is, through Christ, to men in such a case as they are, who are yet estranged from him. And, indeed, I did often say in my heart before the Lord, That if to be hanged up presently before their eyes would be a means to awaken them, and confirm them in the truth, I gladly should be contented.

282. For I have been in my preaching, especially when I have been engaged in the doctrine of life by Christ, without works, as if an angel of God had stood by at my back to encourage me. Oh, it hath been with such power and heavenly evidence upon my own soul, while I have been labouring to unfold it, to demonstrate it, and to fasten it upon the consciences of others, that I could not be contented with saying, I believe, and am sure; methought I was more than sure, if it be lawful so to

express myself, that those things which then I asserted were true.

283. When I went first to preach the Word abroad, the doctors and priests of the country did open wide against me. But I was persuaded of this, not to render railing for railing, but to see how many of their carnal professors I could convince of their miserable state by the law, and of the want and worth of Christ; for, thought I, This shall answer for me in time to come, when they shall be for my hire before their faces (*Gen. xxx. 33*).

284. I never cared to meddle with things that were controverted, and in dispute amongst the saints, especially things of the lowest nature; yet it pleased me much to contend with great earnestness for the word of faith and the remission of sins by the death and sufferings of Jesus; but I say, as to other things, I should let them alone, because I saw they engendered strife, and because that they neither, in doing nor in leaving undone, did commend us to God to be his. Besides, I saw my work before me did run in another channel even to carry an awakening word; to that therefore did I stick and adhere.

285. I never endeavoured to, nor durst make use of other men's lines (*Rom. xv. 18*), though I condemn not all that do, for I verily thought, and found by experience, that what was taught me by the Word and Spirit of Christ, could be spoken, maintained, and stood to by the soundest and best established conscience; and though I will not now speak all that I know in this matter, yet my experience hath more interest in that text of Scripture than many amongst men are aware (*Gal. i. 11, 12*).

286. If any of those who were awakened by my ministry did after that fall back, as sometimes too many did, I can truly say their loss hath been more to me than if one of my own children, begotten of my body, had been going to its grave; I think, verily, I may speak it without an offence to the Lord, nothing hath gone so near me as that, unless it was the fear of the loss of the salvation of my own soul. I have counted as if I had goodly buildings and lordships in those places where my children were born; my heart hath been so wrapped up in the glory of

this excellent work, that I counted myself more blessed and honoured of God by this than if he had made me the emperor of the Christian world, or the lord of all the glory of the earth without it! O these words, "He which converteth the sinner from the error of his way shall save a soul from death" (*Jas. v. 20*). "The fruit of the righteous *is* a tree of life; and he that winneth souls *is* wise" (*Prov. xi. 30*). "They that be wise shall shine as the brightness of the firmament; and they that turn many to righteousness as the stars for ever and ever" (*Dan. xii. 3*). "For what is our hope, or joy, or crown of rejoicing? *Are* not even ye in the presence of our Lord Jesus Christ at his coming? For ye are our glory and joy" (*1 Thess. ii. 19, 20*). These, I say, with many others of a like nature, have been great refreshments to me.

287. I have observed, that where I have had a work to do for God, I have had first, as it were, the going of God upon my spirit to desire I might preach there. I have also observed that such and such souls in particular have been strongly set upon my heart, and I stirred up to wish for their salvation; and that these very souls have, after this, been given in as the fruits of my ministry. I have also observed, that a word cast in by the by hath done more execution in a sermon than all that was spoken besides; sometimes also when I have thought I did no good, then I did the most of all; and at other times when I thought I should catch them I have fished for nothing.

288. I have also observed, that where there hath been a work to do upon sinners, there the devil hath begun to roar in the hearts, and by the mouths of his servants. Yea, oftentimes when the wicked world hath raged most, there hath been souls awaked by the Word. I could instance particulars, but I forbear.

289. My great desire in my fulfilling my ministry was to get into the darkest places of the country, even amongst those people that were farthest off of profession; yet not because I could not endure the light, for I feared not to show my gospel to any, but because I found my spirit leaned most after awakening and converting work, and the Word that I carried did lead itself most that way

also; "yea, so have I strived to preach the gospel, not where Christ was named, lest I should build upon another man's foundation" (*Rom. xv. 20*).

290. In my preaching I have really been in pain, and have, as it were, travailed to bring forth children to God; neither could I be satisfied unless some fruits did appear in my work. If I were fruitless it mattered not who commended me; but if I were fruitful, I cared not who did condemn. I have thought of that, "He that winneth souls *is* wise" (*Prov. xi. 30*); and again, "Lo, children *are* an heritage of the Lord; *and* the fruit of the womb *is his* reward. As arrows in the hand of a mighty man, so *are* children of the youth. Happy *is* the man that hath filled his quiver full of them; they shall not be ashamed, but they shall speak with the enemies in the gate" (*Ps. cxxvii. 3–5*).

291. It pleased me nothing to see people drink in opinions if they seemed ignorant of Jesus Christ, and the worth of their own salvation, sound conviction of sin, especially for unbelief, and an heart set on fire to be saved by Christ, with strong breathing after a truly sanctified soul; that it was that delighted me; those were the souls I counted blessed.

292. But in this work, as in all other, I had my temptations attending me, and that of diverse kinds, as sometimes I should be assaulted with great discouragement therein, fearing that I should not be able to speak the Word at all to edification; nay, that I should not be able to speak sense unto the people; at which times I should have such a strange faintness and strengthlessness seize upon my body that my legs have scarce been able to carry me to the place of exercise.

293. Sometimes, again, when I have been preaching, I have been violently assaulted with thoughts of blasphemy, and strongly tempted to speak the words with my mouth before the congregation. I have also at some times, even when I have begun to speak the Word with much clearness, evidence, and liberty of speech, yet been before the ending of that opportunity so blinded, and so estranged from the things I have been speaking,

and have also been so straitened in my speech, as to utterance before the people, that I have been as if I had not known or remembered what I have been about, or as if my head had been in a bag all the time of the exercise.

294. Again, when as sometimes I have been about to preach upon some smart and scorching portion of the Word, I have found the tempter suggest, What, will you preach this? this condemns yourself; of this your own soul is guilty; wherefore preach not of it at all; or if you do, yet so mince it as to make way for your own escape; lest instead of awakening others, you lay that guilt upon your own soul, as you will never get from under.

295. But, I thank the Lord, I have been kept from consenting to these so horrid suggestions, and have rather, as Samson, bowed myself with all my might, to condemn sin and transgression wherever I found it, yea, though therein also I did bring guilt upon my own conscience! "Let me die," thought I, "with the Philistines" (*Judges xvi. 29, 30*), rather than deal corruptly with the blessed Word of God, "Thou that teachest another, teachest not thou thyself?" It is far better that thou do judge thyself, even by preaching plainly to others, than that thou, to save thyself, imprison the truth in unrighteousness; blessed be God for his help also in this.

296. I have also, while found in this blessed work of Christ, been often tempted to pride and liftings up of heart; and though I dare not say I have not been infected with this, yet truly the Lord, of his precious mercy, hath so carried it towards me, that, for the most part, I have had but small joy to give way to such a thing; for it hath been my every day's portion to be let into the evil of my own heart, and still made to see such a multitude of corruptions and infirmities therein, that it hath caused hanging down of the head under all my gifts and attainments; I have felt this thorn in the flesh, the very mercy of God to me (*2 Cor. xii. 7–9*).

297. I have had also, together with this, some notable place or other of the Word presented before me, which word hath contained in it some sharp and piercing

sentence concerning the perishing of the soul, notwithstanding gifts and parts; as, for instance, that hath been
of great use unto me, "Though I speak with the tongues
of men and of angels, and have not charity, I am become
as sounding brass, and a tinkling cymbal" (*1 Cor. xiii. 1,
2*).

298. A tinkling cymbal is an instrument of music, with
which a skilful player can make such melodious and
heart-inflaming music, that all who hear him play can
scarcely hold from dancing; and yet behold the cymbal
hath not life, neither comes the music from it, but
because of the art of him that plays therewith; so then the
instrument at last may come to naught and perish,
though, in times past, such music hath been made upon
it.

299. Just thus I saw it was and will be with them who
have gifts, but want saving grace, they are in the hand of
Christ, as the cymbal in the hand of David; and as David
could, with the cymbal, make that mirth in the service of
God, as to elevate the hearts of the worshippers, so
Christ can use these gifted men, as with them to affect
the souls of his people in his church; yet when he hath
done all, hang them by as lifeless, though sounding
cymbals.

300. This consideration, therefore, together with some
others, were, for the most part, as a maul on the head of
pride, and desire of vain glory; what, thought I, shall I be
proud because I am a sounding brass? Is it so much to be
a fiddle? Hath not the least creature that hath life, more
of God in it than these? Besides, I knew it was love
should never die, but these must cease and vanish; so I
concluded, a little grace, a little love, a little of the true
fear of God, is better than all these gifts; yea, and I am
fully convinced of it, that it is possible for a soul that can
scarce give a man an answer, but with great confusion as
to method, I say it is possible for them to have a
thousand times more grace, and so to be more in the love
and favour of the Lord than some who, by virtue of the
gift of knowledge, can deliver themselves like angels.

301. Thus, therefore, I came to perceive, that though

gifts in themselves were good to the thing for which they
are designed, to wit, the edification of others; yet empty
and without power to save the soul of him that hath
them, if they be alone; neither are they, as so, any sign
of a man's state to be happy, being only a dispensation
of God to some, of whose improvement, or non-
improvement, they must, when a little love more is over,
give an account to him that is ready to judge the quick
and the dead.

302. This showed me, too, that gifts being alone, were
dangerous, not in themselves, but because of those evils
that attend them that have them, to wit, pride, desire of
vain glory, self-conceit, etc., all which were easily blown
up at the applause and commendation of every unadvised Christian, to the endangering of a poor creature
to fall into the condemnation of the devil.

303. I saw therefore that he that hath gifts had need be
let into a sight of the nature of them, to wit, that they
come short of making of him to be in a truly saved
condition, lest he rest in them, and so fall short of the
grace of God.

304. He hath also cause to walk humbly with God, and
be little in his own eyes, and to remember withal, that his
gifts are not his own, but the church's; and that by them
he is made a servant to the church; and he must give at
last an account of his stewardship unto the Lord Jesus;
and to give a good account, will be a blessed thing.

305. Let all men therefore prize a little with the fear of
the Lord; gifts indeed are desirable, but yet great grace
and small gifts are better than great gifts and no grace. It
doth not say, the Lord gives gifts and glory, but the Lord
gives grace and glory; and blessed is such an one to
whom the Lord gives grace, true grace, for that is a
certain forerunner of glory.

306. But when Satan perceived that his thus tempting
and assaulting of me would not answer his design, to wit,
to overthrow my ministry, and make it ineffectual, as to
the ends thereof; then he tried another way, which was to
stir up the minds of the ignorant and malicious, to load
me with slanders and reproaches; now therefore I may

say, that what the devil could devise and his instruments invent, was whirled up and down the country against me, thinking, as I said, that by that means they should make my ministry to be abandoned.

307. It began therefore to be rumoured up and down among the people, that I was a witch, a jesuit, a highwayman, and the like.

308. To all which, I shall only say, God knows that I am innocent. But as for mine accusers, let them provide themselves to meet me before the tribunal of the Son of God, there to answer for all these things, with all the rest of their iniquities, unless God shall give them repentance for them, for the which I pray with all my heart.

309. But that which was reported with the boldest confidence, was, that I had my misses, my whores, my bastards, yea, two wives at once, and the like. Now these slanders, with the other, I glory in, because but slanders, foolish, or knavish lies, and falsehoods cast upon me by the devil and his seed; and should I not be dealt with thus wickedly by the world, I should want one sign of a saint, and a child of God. "Blessed are ye (said the Lord Jesus) when men shall revile you, and persecute you, and shall say all manner of evil against you falsely for my sake; rejoice, and be exceeding glad, for great *is* your reward in heaven; for so persecuted they the prophets which were before you" (*Matt. v. 11*).

310. These things, therefore, upon mine own account, trouble me not; no, though they were twenty times more than they are. I have a good conscience, and whereas they speak evil of me, as an evil doer, they shall be ashamed that falsely accuse my good conversation in Christ.

311. So then, what shall I say to those that have thus bespattered me? Shall I threaten them? Shall I chide them? Shall I flatter them? Shall I intreat them to hold their tongues? No, not I, were it not for that these things make them ripe for damnation, that are the authors and abettors, I would say unto them, Report it, because it will increase my glory.

312. Therefore I bind these lies and slanders to me as

an ornament, it beongs to my Christian profession to be vilified, slandered, reproached and reviled; and since all this is nothing else, as my God and my conscience do bear me witness, I rejoice in reproaches for Christ's sake.

313. I also calling all those fools, or knaves, that have thus made it anything of their business to affirm any of the things afore-named of me, namely, that I have been naught with other women, or the like. When they have used to the utmost of their endeavours, and made the fullest inquiry that they can, to prove against me truly, that there is any woman in heaven, or earth, or hell, that can say, I have at any time, in any place, by day or night, so much as attempted to be naught with them; and speak I thus, to beg mine enemies into a good esteem of me? no, not I: I will in this beg relief of no man; believe or disbelieve me in this, all is a case to me.

314. My foes have missed their mark in this their shooting at me. I am not the man. I wish that they themselves be guiltless. If all the fornicators and adulterers in England were hanged by the neck till they be dead, JOHN BUNYAN, the object of their envy, would be still alive and well. I know not whether there be such a thing as a woman breathing under the copes of the whole heaven, but by their apparel, their children, or by common fame, except my wife.

315. And in this I admire the wisdom of God, that he made me shy of women from my first conversion until now. Those know, and can also bear me witness, with whom I have been most intimately concerned, that it is a rare thing to see me carry it pleasant towards a woman; the common salutation of a woman I abhor, it is odious to me in whomsoever I see it. Their company alone, I cannot away with. I seldom so much as touch a woman's hand, for I think these things are not so becoming me. When I have seen good men salute those women that they have visited, or that have visited them, I have at times made my objection against it, and when they have answered, that it was but a piece of civility, I have told them, it is not a comely sight; some indeed have urged the holy kiss; but then I have asked why they made

baulks, why they did salute the most handsome, and let the illfavoured go; thus, how laudable soever such things have been in the eyes of others, they have been unseemly in my sight.

316. And now for a wind up in this matter, I calling not only men, but angels, to prove me guilty of having carnally to do with any woman save my wife, nor am I afraid to do it a second time, knowing that I cannot offend the Lord in such a case, to call God for a record upon my soul, that in these things I am innocent. Not that I have been thus kept, because of any goodness in me more than any other, but God has been merciful to me, and has kept me; to whom I pray that he will keep me still, not only from this, but from every evil way and work, and preserve me to his heavenly kingdom. *Amen.*

317. Now as Satan laboured by reproaches and slanders, to make me vile among my countrymen, that, if possible, my preaching might be made of none effect, so there was added hereto a long and tedious imprisonment, that thereby I might be frighted from my service for Christ, and the world terrified, and made afraid to hear me preach, of which I shall in the next place give you a brief account.

A BRIEF ACCOUNT OF THE AUTHOR'S IMPRISONMENT

318. Having made profession of the glorious gospel of Christ a long time, and preached the same about five years, I was apprehended at a meeting of good people in the country, among whom, had they let me alone, I should have preached that day, but they took me away from amongst them, and had me before a justice; who, after I had offered security for my appearing at the next sessions, yet committed me, because my sureties would not consent to be bound that I should preach no more to the people.

319. At the sessions after, I was indicted for an upholder and maintainer of unlawful assemblies and

conventicles, and for not conforming to the national worship of the Church of England; and after some conference there with the justices, they taking my plain dealing with them for a confession, as they termed it, of the indictment, did sentence me to perpetual banishment, because I refused to conform. So being again delivered up to the jailer's hands, I was had home to prison again, and there have lain now complete twelve years, waiting to see what God would suffer these men to do with me.

320. In which condition I have continued with much content, through grace, but have met with many turnings and goings upon my heart, both from the Lord, Satan, and my own corruptions; by all which, glory be to Jesus Christ, I have also received among many things, much conviction, instruction, and understanding, of which at large I shall not here discourse; only give you in a hint or two, a word that may stir up the godly to bless God, and to pray for me; and also to take encouragement, should the case be their own, not to fear what man can do unto them.

321. I never had in all my life so great an inlet into the Word of God as now; those Scriptures that I saw nothing in before, are made in this place and state to shine upon me; Jesus Christ also was never more real and apparent than now; here I have seen him and felt him indeed: O that word, We have not preached unto you cunningly devised fables (*2 Pet. i. 16*); and that, God raised Christ from the dead, and gave him glory, that your faith and hope might be in God (*1 Pet. i. 21*), were blessed words unto me in this my imprisoned condition.

322. These three or four scriptures also have been great refreshment in this condition to me: *John xiv. 1-4; John xvi. 33; Col. iii. 3, 4; Heb. xii. 22-4.* So that sometimes when I have been in the savour of them, I have been able to laugh at destruction, and to fear neither the horse nor his rider (*Job xxxix. 18*). I have had sweet sights of the forgiveness of my sins in this place, and of my being with Jesus in another world: O, "the mount Zion, the heavenly Jerusalem, the innumerable

company of angels, and God the judge of all, and the spirits of just men made perfect, and to Jesus" (*Heb. xii. 22–4*), have been sweet unto me in this place: I have seen THAT here, that I am persuaded I shall never, while in this world, be able to express; I have seen a truth in that scripture, "Whom having not seen, ye love; in whom, though now ye see *him* not, yet believing, ye rejoice with joy unspeakable and full of glory" (*1 Pet. i. 8*).

323. I never knew what it was for God to stand by me at all turns, and at every offer of Satan to afflict me, etc., as I have found him since I came in hither; for look how fears have presented themselves, so have supports and encouragements, yea, when I have started, even as it were at nothing else but my shadow, yet God, as being very tender of me, hath not suffered me to be molested, but would with one scripture and another strengthen me against all; insomuch that I have often said, Were it lawful, I could pray for greater trouble, for the greater comfort's sake (*Eccles. vii. 14; 2 Cor. i. 5*).

324. Before I came to prison, I saw what was a-coming, and had especially two considerations warm upon my heart; the first was how to be able to endure, should my imprisonment be long and tedious; the second was how to be able to encounter death, should that be here my portion; for the first of these, that scripture, *Col. i. 11*, was great information to me, namely, to pray to God to be "strengthened with all might, according to his glorious power, unto all patience and longsuffering with joyfulness." I could seldom go to prayer before I was imprisoned, but not for so little as a year together, this sentence, or sweet petition, would, as it were, thrust itself into my mind, and persuade me, that if ever I would go through long-suffering, I must have all patience, especially if I would endure it joyfully.

325. As to the second consideration, that saying, *2 Cor. i. 9*, was of great use to me, "But we had the sentence of death in ourselves, that we should not trust in ourselves, but in God which raiseth the dead." By this scripture I was made to see, that if ever I would suffer rightly, I must first pass a sentence of death upon everything that

can properly be called a thing of this life, even to reckon myself, my wife, my children, my health, my enjoyments, and all, as dead to me, and myself as dead to them. "He that loveth father or mother, son or daughter, more than me, is not worthy of me" (*Matt. x. 37*).

326. The second was, to live upon God that is invisible; as Paul said in another place, the way not to faint, is to "look not at the things which are seen, but at the things which are not seen: for the things which are seen *are* temporal; but the things which are not seen *are* eternal" (*2 Cor. iv. 18*). And thus I reasoned with myself; if I provide only for a prison, then the whip comes at unawares; and so does also the pillory; again, if I provide only for these, then I am not fit for banishment; further, if I conclude that banishment is the worst, then if death come I am surprised. So that I see the best way to go through sufferings is to trust in God through Christ, as touching the world to come; and as touching this world, to count "the grave my house, to make my bed in darkness, and to say to corruption, Thou *art* my father, and to the worm, *Thou art* my mother and my sister." That is, to familiarise these things to me.

327. But notwithstanding these helps, I found myself a man, and compassed with infirmities; the parting with my wife and poor children hath oft been to me in this place as the pulling the flesh from my bones, and that not only because I am somewhat too too fond of those great mercies, but also because I should have often brought to my mind the many hardships, miseries and wants that my poor family was like to meet with, should I be taken from them, especially my poor blind child, who lay nearer my heart than all I had besides; O the thoughts of the hardship I thought my blind one might go under, would break my heart to pieces.

328. Poor child, thought I, what sorrow art thou like to have for thy portion in this world? Thou must be beaten, must beg, suffer hunger, cold, nakedness, and a thousand calamities, though I cannot now endure the wind should blow upon thee. But yet recalling myself, thought I, I must venture you all with God, though it goeth to the

quick to leave you. Oh, I saw in this condition I was as a man who was pulling down his house upon the head of his wife and children; yet thought I, I must do it, I must do it. And now I thought on those two milch kine that were to carry the ark of God into another country, and to leave their calves behind them (*1 Sam. vi. 10–12*).

329. But that which helped me in this temptation was divers considerations, of which three in special here I will name; the first was the consideration of those two scriptures, "Leave thy fatherless children, I will preserve *them* alive, and let thy widows trust in me"; and again, "The Lord said, Verily it shall *be* well with thy remnant; verily I will cause the enemy to entreat thee *well* in the time of evil," etc. (*Jer. xlix. 11; xv. 11*).

330. I had also this consideration, that if I should now venture all for God, I engaged God to take care of my concernments; but if I forsook him and his ways, for fear of any trouble that should come to me or mine, then I should not only falsify my profession, but should count also that my concernments were not so sure, if left at God's feet, while I stood to and for his name, as they would be, if they were under my own tuition, though with the denial of the way of God. This was a smarting consideration, and was as spurs unto my flesh. That scripture also greatly helped it to fasten the more upon me, where Christ prays against Judas, that God would disappoint him in all his selfish thoughts, which moved him to sell his master: pray read it soberly, *Ps. cix. 6–20*.

331. I had also another consideration, and that was, the dread of the torments of hell, which I was sure they must partake of, that for fear of the cross, do shrink from their profession of Christ, his words, and laws, before the sons of men: I thought also of the glory that he had prepared for those that, in faith, and love, and patience, stood to his ways before them. These things, I say, have helped me, when the thoughts of the misery that both myself and mine, might for the sake of my profession be exposed to, hath lain pinching on my mind.

332. When I have indeed conceited that I might be banished for my profession, then I have thought of that

scripture, "They were stoned, they were sawn asunder, were tempted, were slain with the sword; they wandered about in sheepskins and goatskins; being destitute, afflicted, tormented, of whom theworld was not worthy" (*Heb. xi. 37*), for all they thought they were too bad to dwell and abide amongst them. I have also thought of that saying, "The Holy Ghost witnesseth in every city, that bounds and afflictions abide me." I have verily thought that my soul and it have sometimes reasoned about the sore and sad estate of a banished and exiled condition, how they are exposed to hunger, to cold, to perils, to nakedness, to enemies, and a thousand calamities; and at last, it may be, to die in a ditch, like a poor forlorn and desolate sheep. But I thank God, hitherto I have not been moved by these most delicate reasonings, but have rather, by them, more approved my heart to God.

333. I will tell you a pretty business; I was once above all the rest in a very sad and low condition for many weeks; at which time also I being but a young prisoner, and not acquainted with the laws, had this lay much upon my spirit, That my imprisonment might end at the gallows for aught that I could tell. Now, therefore, Satan laid hard at me to beat me out of heart, by suggesting thus unto me, But how if when you come indeed to die, you should be in this condition; that is, as not to savour the things of God, nor to have any evidence upon your soul for a better state hereafter? For indeed at that time all the things of God were hid from my soul.

334. Wherefore, when I at first began to think of this, it was a great trouble to me; for I thought with myself, that in the condition I now was in, I was not fit to die, neither indeed did think I could, if I should be called to it: besides, I thought with myself, if I should make a scrabbling shift to clamber up the ladder, yet I should either with quaking, or other symptoms of faintings, give occasion to the enemy to reproach the way of God and his people, for their timorousness. This therefore lay with great trouble upon me, for methought I was ashamed to die with a pale face, and tottering knees, for such a cause as this.

335. Wherefore, I prayed to God that he would comfort me, and give me strength to do and suffer what he should call me to; yet no comfort appeared, but all continued hid: I was also at this time so really possessed with the thought of death, that oft I was as if I was on the ladder with a rope about my neck; only this was some encouragement to me, I thought I might now have an opportunity to speak my last words to a multitude, which I thought would come to see me die; and, thought I, if it must be so, if God will but convert one soul by my very last words, I shall not count my life thrown away, nor lost.

336. But yet all the things of God were kept out of my sight, and still the tempter followed me with, But whither must you go when you die? What will become of you? Where will you be found in another world? What evidence have you for heaven and glory, and an inheritance among them that are sanctified? Thus was I tossed for many weeks, and knew not what to do; at last this consideration fell with weight upon me, That it was for the Word and way of God that I was in this condition, wherefore I was engaged not to flinch a hair's breadth from it.

337. I thought also, that God might choose whether he would give me comfort now or at the hour of death, but I might not therefore choose whether I would hold my profession or no: I was bound, but he was free: yea, it was my duty to stand to his word, whether he would ever look upon me or no, or save me at the last: wherefore, thought I, the point being thus, I am for going on, and venturing my eternal state with Christ, whether I have comfort here or no; if God doth not come in, thought I, I will leap off the ladder even blindfold into eternity, sink or swim, come heaven, come hell, Lord Jesus, if thou wilt catch me, do; if not, I will venture for thy name.

338. I was no sooner fixed upon this resolution, but that word dropped upon me, "Doth Job serve God for naught?" As if the accuser had said, Lord, Job is no upright man, he serves thee for by-respects: hast thou not made a hedge about him, etc. "But put forth thine hand

now, and touch all that he hath, and he will curse thee to thy face." How now, thought I, is this the sign of an upright soul, to desire to serve God, that will serve God for nothing rather than give out? Blessed be God, then, I hope I have an upright heart, for I am resolved, God giving me strength, never to deny my profession, though I have nothing at all for my pains; and as I was thus considering, that scripture was set before me, *Ps. xliv. 12–26.*

339. Now was my heart full of comfort, for I hoped it was sincere: I would not have been without this trial for much; I am comforted every time I think of it, and I hope I shall bless God for ever for the teaching I have had by it. Many more of the dealings of God towards me I might relate, but these, "Out of the spoils won in battles have I dedicated to maintain the house of the Lord" (*1 Chron, xxvi. 27*).

THE CONCLUSION

1. Of all the temptations that ever I met with in my life, to question the being of God, and truth of his gospel, is the worst, and the worst to be borne; when this temptation comes, it takes away my girdle from me, and removeth the foundation from under me. Oh, I have often thought of that word, "Have your loins girt about with truth"; and of that, "When the foundations are destroyed, what can the righteous do?"

2. Sometimes, when, after sin committed, I have looked for sore chastisement from the hand of God, the very next that I have had from him hath been the discovery of his grace. Sometimes, when I have been comforted, I have called myself a fool for my so sinking under trouble. And then, again, when I have been cast down, I thought I was not wise to give such way to comfort. With such strength and weight have both these been upon me.

3. I have wondered much at this one thing, that though God doth visit my soul with never so blessed a

discovery of himself, yet I have found again, that such hours have attended me afterwards, that I have been in my spirit, so filled with darkness, that I could not so much as once conceive what that God and that comfort was with which I have been refreshed.

4. I have sometimes seen more in a line of the Bible than I could well tell how to stand under, and yet at another time the whole Bible hath been to me as dry as a stick; or rather, my heart hath been so dead and dry unto it, that I could not conceive the least drachm of refreshment, though I have looked it all over.

5. Of all tears, they are the best that are made by the blood of Christ; and of all joy, that is the sweetest that is mixed with mourning over Christ. Oh! it is a goodly thing to be on our knees, with Christ in our arms, before God. I hope I know something of these things.

6. I find to this day seven abominations in my heart: (1) Inclinings to unbelief. (2) Suddenly to forget the love and mercy that Christ manifesteth. (3) A leaning to the works of the law. (4) Wanderings and coldness in prayer. (5) To forget to watch for that I pray for. (6) Apt to murmur because I have no more, and yet ready to abuse what I have. (7) I can do none of those things which God commands me, but my corruptions will thrust in themselves, "When I would do good, evil is present with me."

7. These things I continually see and feel, and am afflicted and oppressed with; yet the widsom of God doth order them for my good. (1) They make me abhor myself. (2) They keep me from trusting my heart. (3) They convince me of the insufficiency of all inherent righteousness. (4) They show me the necessity of flying to Jesus. (5) They press me to pray unto God. (6) They show me the need I have to watch and be sober. (7) And provoke me to look to God, through Christ, to help me, and carry me through this world. Amen.

A Relation of the Imprisonment of Mr. John Bunyan, Minister of the Gospel at Bedford, in November 1660. His examination before the Justices; his Conference with the Clerk of the Peace; what passed between the Judges and his Wife when she presented a Petition for his Deliverance, etc.

The relation of my imprisonment in the month of November 1660, when, by the good hand of my God, I had for five or six years together, without any interruption, freely preached the blessed gospel of our Lord Jesus Christ; and had also, through his blessed grace, some encouragement by his blessing thereupon; the devil, that old enemy of man's salvation, took his opportunity to inflame the hearts of his vassals against me, insomuch that at the last I was laid out for by the warrant of a justice, and was taken and committed to prison. The relation thereof is as followeth:

Upon the 12th of this instant November 1660, I was desired by some of the friends in the country to come to teach at Samsell, by Harlington, in Bedfordshire. To whom I made a promise, if the Lord permitted, to be with them on the time aforesaid. The justic hearing thereof, whose name is Mr. Francis Wingate, forthwith issued out his warrant to take me, and bring me before him, and in the meantime to keep a very strong watch about the house where the meeting should be kept, as if we that were to meet together in that place did intend to do some fearful business, to the destruction of the country; when, alas, the constable, when he came in, found us only with our Bibles in our hands, ready to speak and hear the Word of God; for we were just about to begin our exercise. Nay, we had begun in prayer for the blessing of God upon our opportunity, intending to have preached the Word of the Lord unto them there present; but the constable coming in prevented us; so that I was taken and forced to depart the room. But had I been minded to have played the coward, I could have escaped, and kept out of his hands. For when I was come to my friend's house, there was whispering that that day I should be taken, for there was a warrant out to take me; which when my friend heard, he being somewhat timorous, questioned whether we had best have our meeting or not; and whether it might not be better for me to depart, lest they should take me and have me before the justice, and after that send me to prison, for he knew better than I what spirit they were of, living by them; to whom I said, No, by no means, I will not stir, neither will I have the meeting dismissed for this. Come, be of good cheer, let us not be daunted; our cause is good, we need not be ashamed of it; to preach God's Word is so good a work, that we shall be well rewarded, if we suffer for that; or to this purpose; but as for my friend, I think he was more afraid of [for] me, than of himself. After this I walked into the close, where, I somewhat seriously considering the matter, this came into my mind, That I had showed myself hearty and courageous in my preaching, and had, blessed be grace, made it my business to encourage others; therefore, thought I, if I should now run, and make an escape, it will be of a very ill savour in the country. For what will my weak and newly converted brethren think of it, but that I was not so strong in deed as I was in word? Also I feared that if I should run, now there was a warrant out for me, I might by so doing make them afraid to stand, when great words only should be spoken to them. Besides, I thought, that seeing God of his mercy should choose me to go upon the forlorn hope in this country; that is, to be the first that should be opposed, for the gospel; if I should fly, it might be a discouragement to the whole body that might follow after. And further, I thought the world thereby would take occasion at my cowardliness, to have blasphemed the gospel, and to have had some ground to suspect worse of me and my profession than I deserved. These things with others considered by me, I came in again to the house, with a full resolution to keep the meeting, and not to go away, though I could have been gone about an hour before the officer apprehended me; but I would not; for I was resolved to see the utmost of what they could say or do unto me. For blessed by the Lord, I knew of no evil that I had said or done. And so, as aforesaid, I began the meeting. But being prevented by the constable's coming in with his warrant to take me, I could not proceed. But before I went away, I spake some few words of counsel and encouragement to the people, declaring to them, that they saw we were prevented of our opportunity to speak and hear the Word of God, and were like to suffer for the same: desiring them that they should not be discouraged, for it was a mercy to suffer upon so good account. For we might have been apprehended as thieves or murderers, or for other wickedness; but blessed be God it was not so, but we suffer as Christians for well doing: and we had better be the persecuted than the persecutors, etc. But the constable and the justice's man waiting on us would not be at quiet till they had me away, and that we departed the house. But because the justice was not at home that day, there was a friend of mine engaged for me to bring me to the constable on the morrow morning. Otherwise the constable must have charged a watch with me, or have secured me some other ways, my crime was so great. So on the next morning we went to the constable, and so to the justice. He asked the constable what we did, where we were met together, and what we had with us? I trow he meant whether we had armour or not; but when the constable told him, that there were only met a few of us together to preach and hear the Word, and no sign of anything else, he could not well tell what to say: yet because he had sent for me, he did adventure to put out a few proposals to me, which were to this effect, namely, What I did there? and why I did not content myself with following my calling? for it was against the law, that such as I should be admitted to do as I did.

JOHN BUNYAN. To which I answered, that the intent of my coming thither, and to other places, was to instruct and counsel people to forsake their sins, and close in with Christ, lest they did miserably perish; and that I could do both these without confusion, to wit, follow my calling, and preach the Word also.

At which words, he was in a chafe, as it appeared; for he said that he would break the neck of our meetings.

BUN. I said, it may be so. Then he wished me to get sureties to be bound for me, or else he would send me to the jail.

My sureties being ready, I called them in, and when the bond for my appearance was made, he told them, that they were bound to keep me from preaching; and that if I did preach, their bonds would be forfeited. To which I answered, that then I should break them; for I should not leave speaking the Word of God: even to counsel, comfort, exhort, and teach the people among whom I came; and I thought this to be a work that had no hurt in it: but was rather worthy of commendation than blame.

WINGATE. Whereat he told me, that if they would not be so bound, my mittimus must be made, and I sent to the jail, there to lie to the quarter-sessions.

Now while my mittimus was making, the justice was withdrawn; and in comes an old enemy to the truth, Dr. Lindale, who, when he was come in, fell to taunting at me with many reviling terms.

BUN. To whom I answered, that I did not come thither to talk with him, but with the justice. Whereat he supposed that I had nothing to say for myself, and triumphed as if he had got the victory; charging and condemning me for meddling with that for which I could show no warrant; and asked me, if I had taken the oaths? and if I had not, it was pity but that I should be sent to prison, etc.

I told him, that if I was minded, I could answer to any sober question that he should put to me. He then urged me again, how I could prove it lawful for me to preach, with a great deal of confidence of the victory.

But at last, because he should see that I could answer him if I listed, I cited to him that verse in Peter, which saith, "As every man hath received the gift, even so let him minister the same," etc.

LIND. Aye, saith he, to whom is that spoken?

BUN. To whom? said I; why, to every man that hath

received a gift from God. Mark, saith the apostle, "As every man that hath received a gift from God," etc. And again, "You may all prophesy one by one." Whereat the man was a little stopt, and went a softlier pace: but not being willing to lose the day, he began again, and said:

LIND. Indeed I do remember that I have read of one Alexander a coppersmith, who did much oppose and disturb the apostles;—aiming, it is like, at me, because I was a tinker.

BUN. To which I answered, that I also had read of very many priests and pharisees that had their hands in the blood of our Lord Jesus Christ.

LIND. Aye, saith he, and you are one of those scribes and pharisees: for you, with a pretence, make long prayers to devour widows' houses.

BUN. I answered, that if he had got no more by preaching and praying than I had done, he would not be so rich as he now was. But that scripture coming into my mind, "Answer not a fool according to his folly," I was as sparing of my speech as I could, without prejudice to truth.

Now by this time my mittimus was made, and I committed to the constable to be sent to the jail in Bedford, etc.

But as I was going, two of my brethren met with me by the way, and desired the constable to stay, supposing that they should prevail with the justice, through the favour of a pretended friend, to let me go at liberty. So we did stay, while they went to the justice; and after much discourse with him, it came to this; that if I would come to him again, and say some certain words to him, I should be released. Which when they told me, I said if the words were such that might be said with a good conscience, I should, or, else, I should not. So through their importunity I went back again, but not believing that I should be delivered: for I feared their spirit was too full of opposition to the truth to let me go, unless I should in something or other dishonour my God, and wound my conscience. Wherefore, as I went, I lifted up my heart to God for light and strength to be kept, that I might not do anything that might either dishonour him, or wrong my own soul, or be a grief or discouragement to any that was inclining after the Lord Jesus Christ.

Well, when I came to the justice again, there was Mr. Foster of Bedford, who coming out of another room, and seeing of me by the light of the candle, for it was dark night when I came thither, he said unto me, Who is there? John Bunyan? with such seeming affection, as if he would have leaped on my neck and kissed me, which made me somewhat wonder, that such a man as he, with whom I had so little acquaintance, and, besides, that had ever been a close opposer of the ways of God, should carry himself so full of love to me; but, afterwards, when I saw what he did, it caused me to remember those sayings, "Their tongues are smoother than oil, but their words are drawn swords." And again, "Beware of men," etc. When I had answered him, that blessed be God I was well, he said, What is the occasion of your being here? or to that purpose. To whom I answered, that I was at a meeting of people a little way off, intending to speak a word of exhortation to them; but the justice hearing thereof, said I, was pleased to send his warrant to fetch me before him, etc.

FOSTER. So, said he, I understand; but well, if you will promise to call the people no more together, you shall have your liberty to go home; for my brother is very loath to send you to prison, if you will be but ruled.

BUN. Sir, said I, pray what do you mean by calling the people together? My business is not anything among them, when they are come together, but to exhort them to look after the salvation of their souls, that they may be saved, etc.

FOST. Saith he, We must not enter into explication or dispute now; but if you will say you will call the people no more together, you may have your liberty; if not, you must be sent away to prison.

BUN. Sir, said, I, I shall not force or compel any man to hear me; but yet, if I come into any place where there is a people met together, I should, according to the best of my skill and wisdom, exhort and counsel them to seek out after the Lord Jesus Christ, for the salvation of their souls.

FOST. He said, that was none of my work; I must follow my calling; and if I would but leave off preaching, and follow my calling, I should have the justice's favour, and be acquitted presently.

BUN. To whom I said, that I could follow my calling and that too, namely, preaching the Word; and I did look upon it as my duty to do them both, as I had an opportunity.

FOST. He said, to have any such meetings was against the law; and, therefore, he would have me leave off, and say I would call the people no more together.

BUN. To whom I said, that I durst not make any further promise; for my conscience would not suffer me to do it. And again, I did look upon it as my duty to do as much good as I could, not only in my trade, but also in communicating to all people, wheresoever I came, the best knowledge I had in the Word.

FOST. He told me that I was the nearest the Papists of any, and that he would convince me of immediately.

BUN. I asked him wherein?

FOST. He said, in that we understood the Scriptures literally.

BUN. I told him that those that were to be understood literally, we understood them so; but for those that were to be understood otherwise, we endeavoured so to understand them.

FOST. He said, Which of the Scriptures do you understand literally?

BUN. I said this, "He that believeth shall be saved." This was to be understood just as it is spoken; that whosoever believeth in Christ shall, according to the plain and simple words of the text, be saved.

FOST. He said that I was ignorant, and did not understand the Scriptures; for how, said he, can you understand them when you know not the original Greek, etc.

BUN. To whom I said, that if that was his opinion, that none could understand the Scriptures but those that had the original Greek, etc., then but a very few of the poorest sort should be saved; this is harsh; yet the Scripture saith, "That God hides these things from the wise and prudent," that is, from the learned of the world, "and reveals them to babes and sucklings."

FOST. He said there were none that heard me but a company of foolish people.

BUN. I told him that there were the wise as well as the foolish that do hear me; and again, those that are most commonly counted foolish by the world are the wisest before God; also, that God had rejected the wise, and mighty, and noble, and chosen the foolish and the base.

FOST. He told me that I made people neglect their calling; and that God had commanded people to work six days, and serve him on the seventh.

BUN. I told him that it was the duty of people, both rich and poor, to look out for their souls on those days as well as for their bodies; and that God would have his people "exhort one another daily, while it is called to-day."

FOST. He said again that there was none but a company of poor. simple, ignorant people that came to hear me.

BUN. I told him that the foolish and ignorant had most need of teaching and information; and, therefore, it would be profitable for me to go on in that work.

FOST. Well, said he, to conclude, but will you promise that you will not call the people together any more? and then you may be released and go home.

BUN. I told him that I durst say no more than I had said; for I durst not leave off that work which God had called me to.

So he withdrew from me, and then came several of the justice's servants to me, and told me that I stood so much upon a nicety. Their master, they said, was willing to let me go; and if I would but say I would call the people no more together, I might have my liberty, etc.

BUN. I told them there were more ways than one in which a man might be said to call the people together. As, for instance, if a man get upon the market-place, and there read a book, or the like, though he do not say to the people, Sirs, come hither and hear; yet if they come to him because he reads, he, by his very reading, may be said to call them together; because they would not have been there to hear if he had not been there to read. And seeing this might be termed a calling the people together, I durst not say I would not call them together; for then, by the same argument, my preaching might be said to call them together.

WING. AND FOST. Then came the justice and Mr. Foster to me again; we had a little more discourse about preaching, but because the method of it is out of my mind, I pass it; and when they saw that I was at a point, and would not be moved nor persuaded,

Mr. Foster, the man that did at the first express so much love to me, told the justice that then he must send me away to prison. And that he would do well, also, if he would present all those that were the cause of my coming among them to meetings. Thus we parted.

And, verily, as I was going forth of the doors, I had much ado to forbear saying to them that I carried the peace of God along with me; but I held my peace, and, blessed be the Lord, went away to prison, with God's comfort in my poor soul.

After I had lain in the jail five or six days, the brethren sought means, again, to get me out by bondsmen; for so ran my mittimus, that I should lie there till I could find sureties. They went to a justice at Elstow, one Mr. Crumpton, to desire him to take bond for my appearing at the quarter-sessions. At the first he told them he would; but afterwards he made a demur at the business, and desired first to see my mittimus, which run to this purpose: That I went about to several conventicles in this country, to the great disparagement of the government of the Church of England, etc. When he had seen it, he said that there might be something more against me than was expressed in my mittimus; and that he was but a young man, and, therefore, he durst not do it. This my jailer told me; whereat I was not at all daunted, but rather glad, and saw evidently that the Lord had heard me; for before I went down to the justice, I begged of

God that if I might do more good by being at liberty than in prison, that then I might be set at liberty; but if not, his will be done; for I was not altogether without hopes but that my imprisonment might be an awakening to the saints in the country, therefore I could not tell well which to choose; only I, in that manner, did commit the thing to God. And verily, at my return, I did meet my God sweetly in the prison again, comforting of me and satisfying of me that it was his will and mind that I should be there.

When I came back again to prison, as I was musing at the slender answer of the justice, this word dropt in upon my heart with some life, "For he knew that for envy they had delivered him."

Thus have I, in short, declared the manner and occasion of my being in prison; where I lie waiting the good will of God, to do with me as he pleaseth; knowing that not one hair of my head can fall to the ground without the will of my Father which is in heaven. Let the rage and malice of men be never so great, they can do no more, nor go no farther, than God permits them; but when they have done their worst, "We know that all things work together for good to them that love God" (*Rom. viii. 28*).

Farewell.

Here is the Sum of my Examination before Justice Keelin, Justice Chester, Justice Blundale, Justice Beecher, and Justice Snagg, etc.

After I had lain in prison above seven weeks, the quarter-sessions was to be kept in Bedford, for the county thereof, unto which I was to be brought; and when my jailer had set me before those justices, there was a bill of indictment preferred against me. The extent thereof was as followeth: "That John Bunyan, of the town of Bedford, labourer, being a person of such and such conditions, he hath, since such a time, devilishly and perniciously abstained from coming to church to hear Divine service, and is a common upholder of several unlawful meetings and conventicles, to the great disturbance and distraction of the good subjects of this kingdom, contrary to the laws of our sovereign lord the King, etc.

THE CLERK. When this was read, the clerk of the sessions said unto me, What say you to this?

BUN. I said, that as to the first part of it, I was a common frequenter of the church of God. And was also, by grace, a member with the people over whom Christ is the Head.

KEELIN. But, saith Justice Keelin, who was the judge in that court? Do you come to church, you know what I mean; to the parish church, to hear Divine service?

BUN. I answered, No, I did not.

KEEL. He asked me why?

BUN. I said, Because I did not find it commanded in the Word of God.

KEEL. He said, We were commanded to pray.

BUN. I said, But not by the Common Prayer Book.

KEEL. He said, How then?

BUN. I said, With the Spirit. As the apostle saith, "I will pray with the Spirit with understanding" (*1 Cor. xiv. 15*).

KEEL. He said, We might pray with the Spirit, and with understanding, and with the Common Prayer Book also.

BUN. I said that the prayers in the Common Prayer Book were such as were made by other men, and not by the motions of the Holy Ghost, within our hearts; and as I said, the apostle saith, he will pray with the Spirit, and with the understanding; not with the Spirit and the Common Prayer Book.

ANOTHER JUSTICE. What do you count prayer? Do you think it is to say a few words over before or among a people?

BUN. I said, No, not so; for men might have many elegant or excellent words, and yet not pray at all; but when a man prayeth, he doth, through a sense of those things which he wants, which sense is begotten by the Spirit, pour out his heart before God through Christ;

though his words be not so many and so excellent as others are.

JUSTICES. They said, That was true.

BUN. I said, This might be done without the Common Prayer Book.

ANOTHER. One of them said (I think it was Justice Blundale, or Justice Snagg), How should we know that you do not write out your prayers first, and then read them afterwards to the people? This he spake in a laughing way.

BUN. I said, It is not our use to take a pen and paper, and write a few words thereon, and then go and read it over to a company of people.

But how should we know it? said he.

BUN. Sir, it is none of our custom, said I.

KEEL. But, said Justice Keelin, it is lawful to use Common Prayer, and such-like forms: for Christ taught his disciples to pray, as John also taught his disciples. And further, said he, cannot one man teach another to pray? "Faith comes by hearing"; and one man may convince another of sin, and therefore prayers made by men, and read over, are good to teach, and help men to pray.

While he was speaking these words, God brought that word into my mind, in the eighth of the Romans, at the 26th verse. I say, God brought it, for I thought not on it before: but as he was speaking, it came so fresh into my mind, and was set so evidently before me, as if the Scripture had said, Take me, take me; so when he had done speaking,

BUN. I said, Sir, the Scripture saith, that it is the Spirit that helpeth our infirmities; for we know not what we should pray for as we ought: but the Spirit itself maketh intercession for us, with sighs and groanings which cannot be uttered. Mark, said I, it doth not say the Common Prayer Book teacheth us how to pray, but the Spirit. And it is "the Spirit that helpeth our infirmities," saith the apostle; he doth not say it is the Common Prayer Book.

And as to the Lord's prayer, although it be an easy

thing to say, "Our Father," etc., with the mouth, yet there are very few that can, in Spirit, say the two first words in that prayer; that is, that can call God their Father, as knowing what it is to be born again, and as having experience, that they are begotten of the Spirit of God; which if they do not, all is but babbling, etc.

KEEL. Justice Keelin said, that that was a truth.

BUN. And I say further, As to your saying that one man may convince another of sin, and that faith comes by hearing, and that one man may tell another how he should pray, etc., I say men may tell each other of their sins, but it is the Spirit that must convince them.

And though it be said that "faith comes by hearing," yet it is the Spirit that worketh faith in the heart through hearing, or else they are not profited by hearing (*Heb. iv. 12*).

And that though one man may tell another how he should pray, yet, as I said before, he cannot pray, nor make his condition known to God, except the Spirit help. It is not the Common Prayer Book that can do this. It is the Spirit that showeth us our sins, and the Spirit that showeth us a Saviour (*John xvi. 16*); and the Spirit that stirreth up in our hearts desires to come to God, for such things as we stand in need of (*Matt. xi. 27*), even sighing out our souls unto him for them with "groans which cannot be uttered." With other words to the same purpose. At this they were set.

KEEL. But, says Justice Keelin, what have you against the Common Prayer Book?

BUN. I said, Sir, if you will hear me, I shall lay down my reasons against it.

KEEL. He said, I should have liberty; but first, said he, let me give you one caution; take heed of speaking irreverently of the Common Prayer Book; for it you do so, you will bring great damage upon yourself.

BUN. So I proceeded, and said, My first reason was, becasue it was not commanded in the Word of God, and therefore I could not use it.

ANOTHER. One of them said, Where do you find it commanded in the Scripture, that you should go to

Elstow, or Bedford, and yet it is lawful to go to either of them is it not?

BUN. I said, To go to Elstow, or Bedford, was a civil thing, and not material, though not commanded, and yet God's Word allowed me to go about my calling and therefore if it lay there, then to go thither, etc. But to pray was a great part of the Divine worship of God, and therefore it ought to be done according to the rule of God's Word.

ANOTHER. One of them said, He will do harm; let him speak no further.

KEEL. Justice Keelin said, No, no, never fear him, we are better established than so; he can do no harm; we know the Common Prayer Book hath been ever since the apostles' time, and is lawful for it to be used in the church.

BUN. I said, Show me the place in the epistles where the Common Prayer Book is written, or one text of Scripture that commands me to read it, and I will use it. But yet, notwithstanding, said I, they that have a mind to use it, they have their liberty; that is, I would not keep them from it; but for our parts, we can pray to God without it. Blessed by his name.

With that, one of them said, Who is your God? Beelzebub? Moreover, they often said that I was possessed with the spirit of delusion, and of the devil. All which sayings I passed over; the Lord forgive them! And further, I said, Blessed be the Lord for it, we are encouraged to meet together, and to pray, and exhort one another; for we have had the comfortable presence of God among us. For ever blessed be his holy name!

KEEL. Justice Keelin called this pedlar's French, saying, that I must leave off my canting. The Lord open his eyes!

BUN. I said, that we ought to "exhort one another daily, while it is called to-day," etc. (*Heb. iii. 13*).

KEEL. Justice Keelin said, that I ought not to preach; and asked me where I had my authority? with other suchlike words.

BUN. I said, that I would prove that it was lawful for me, and such as I am, to preach the Word of God.

KEEL. He said unto me, By what scripture?

I said, By that in the first epistle of *Peter, chap. iv.*, the 10th verse, and *Acts cviii.*, with other scriptures, which he would not suffer me to mention. But said, Hold; not so many, which is the first?

BUN. I said, This: "As every man hath received the gift, *even so* minister the same one to another, as good stewards of the manifold grace of God. If any man speak, *let him speak* as the oracles of God," etc.

KEEL. He said, Let me a little open that scripture to you: "As every man hath received the gift"; that is, said he, as everyone hath received a trade, so let him follow it. If any man have received a gift of tinkering, as thou hast done, let him follow his tinkering. And so other men their trades; and the divine his calling, etc.

BUN. Nay, sir, said I, but it is most clear, that the apostle speaks here of preaching the Word; if you do but compare both the verses together, the next verse explains this gift what it is, saying, "If any man speak, *let him speak* as the oracles of God." So that it is plain, that the Holy Ghost doth not so much in this place exhort to civil callings, as to the exercising of those gifts that we have received from God. I would have gone on, but he would not give me leave.

KEEL. He said, We might do it in our families, but not otherwise.

BUN. I said, If it was lawful to do good to some, it was lawful to do good to more. If it was a good duty to exhort our families, it is good to exhort others; but if they held it a sin to meet together to seek the face of God, and exhort one another to follow Christ, I should sin still; for so we should do.

KEEL. He said he was not so well versed in Scripture as to dispute, or words to that purpose. And said, moreover, that they could not wait upon me any longer; but said to me, Then you confess the indictment, do you not? Now, and not till now, I saw was indicted.

BUN. I said, This I confess, we have had many meetings together, both to pray to God, and to exhort one another, and that we had the sweet comforting presence of the Lord among us for our encouragement; blessed be his name therefor. I confessed myself guilty no otherwise.

KEEL. Then, said he, hear your judgment. You must be had back again to prison, and there lie for three months following; and at three months' end, if you do not submit to go to church to hear Divine service, and leave your preaching, you must be banished the realm: and if, after such a day as shall be appointed you to be gone, you shall be found in this realm, etc., or be found to come over again without special licence from the king, etc., you must stretch by the neck for it, I tell you plainly; and so he bid my jailer have me away.

BUN. I told him, as to this matter, I was at a point with him; for if I was out of prison to-day I would preach the gospel again to-morrow, by the help of God.

ANOTHER. To which one made me some answer; but my jailer pulling me away to be gone, I could not tell what he said.

Thus I departed from them; and I can truly say, I bless the Lord Jesus Christ for it, that my heart was sweetly refreshed in the time of my examination; and also afterwards, at my returning to the prison. So that I found Christ's words more than bare trifles, where he saith, "I will give you a mouth and wisdom, which all your adversaries shall not be able to gainsay nor resist" (*Luke xxi. 15*). And that his peace no man can take from us.

Thus have I given you the substance of my examination. The Lord make these profitable to all that shall read or hear them. Farewell.

The Substance of some Discourse had between the Clerk of the Peace and myself, when he came to admonish me, according to the tenor of that Law by which I was in Prison

When I had lain in prison other twelve weeks, and now not knowing what they intended to do with me, upon the 3rd of April, 1661, comes Mr. Cobb unto me, as he told me, being sent by the justices to admonish me; and demanded of me submittance to the Church of England, etc. The extent of our discourse was as followeth:

COBB. When he was come into the house he sent for me out of my chamber; who, when I was come unto him, he said, Neighbour Bunyan, how do you do?

BUN. I thank you, sir, said I, very well, blessed be the Lord.

COBB. Saith he, I come to tell you that it is desired you would submit yourself to the laws of the land, or else at the next sessions it will go worse with you, even to be sent away out of the nation, or else worse than that.

BUN. I said that I did desire to demean myself in the world, both as becometh a man and a Christian.

COBB. But, saith he, you must submit to the laws of the land, and leave off those meetings which you was wont to have; for the statute law is directly against it; and I am sent to you by the justices to tell you that they do intend to prosecute the law against you if you submit not.

BUN. I said, Sir, I conceive that that law by which I am in prison at this time doth not reach or condemn either me or the meetings which I do frequent; that law was made against those that, being designed to do evil in their meetings, make the exercise of religion their pretence, to cover their wickedness. It doth not forbid the private meetings of those that plainly and simply make it their only end to worship the Lord, and to exhort one another to edification. My end in meeting with others is simply to do as much good as I can by exhortation and counsel, according to that small measure of light which God hath given me, and not to disturb the peace of the nation.

COBB. Everyone will say the same, said he; you see the late insurrection at London, under what glorious pretences they went; and yet, indeed, they intended no less than the ruin of the kingdom and commonwealth.

BUN. That practice of theirs I abhor, said I; yet it doth not follow that, because they did so, therefore all others will do so. I look upon it as my duty to behave myself under the king's government, both as beomes a man and a Christian, and if an occasion were offered me, I should willingly manifest my loyalty to my prince, both in word and deed.

COBB. Well, said he, I do not profess myself to be a man that can dispute; but this I say, truly, neighbour Bunyan, I would have you consider this matter seriously, and submit yourself; you may have your liberty to exhort your neighbour in private discourse, so be you do not call together an assembly of people; and, truly, you may do much good to the church of Christ, if you would go this way; and this you may do, and the law not abridge you of it. It is your private meetings that the law is against.

BUN. Sir, said I, if I may do good to one by my discourse, why may I not do good to two? and if to two, why not to four, and so to eight? etc.

COBB. Aye, saith he, and to a hundred, I warrant you.

BUN. Yes, sir, said I, I think I should not be forbid to do as much good as I can.

COBB. But, saith he, you may but pretend to do good, and indeed, notwithstanding, do harm, by seducing the people; you are, therefore, denied your meeting so many together, lest you should do harm.

BUN. And yet, said I, you say the law tolerates me to discourse with my neighbour; surely there is no law tolerates me to seduce anyone; therefore, if I may, by the law, discourse with one, surely it is to do him good; and if I, by discoursing, may do good to one, surely, by the same law, I may do good to many.

COBB. The law, saith he, doth expressly forbid your private meetings; therefore they are not to be tolerated.

BUN. I told him that I would not entertain so much uncharitableness of that Parliament in the 35th of Elizabeth, or of the queen herself, as to think they did, by that law, intend the oppressing of any of God's ordinances, or the interrupting any in the way of God; but men may, in the wresting of it, turn it against the way of God; but take the law in itself, and it only fighteth against those that drive at mischief in their hearts and meetings, making religion only their cloak, colour, or pretence; for so are the words of the satute: "If any meetings, under colour or pretence of religion," etc.

COBB. Very good; therefore the king, seeing that pretences are usually in and among people, as to make religion their pretence only, therefore he, and the law before him, doth forbid such private meetings, and tolerates only public; you may meet in public.

BUN. Sir, said I, let me answer you in a similitude: Set the case that, at such a wood corner, there did usually come forth thieves, to do mischief; must there therefore a law be made that everyone that cometh out there shall be killed? May there not come out true men as well as thieves out from thence? Just thus it is in this case; I do think they may be many that may design the destruction of the commonwealth; but it does not follow therefore that all private meetings are unlawful; those that transgress, let them be punished. And if at any time I myself should do any act in my conversation as doth not become a man and Christian, let me bear the punishment. And as for your saying I may meet in public, if I may be suffered, I would gladly do it. Let me have but meeting enough in public, and I shall care the less to have them in private. I do not meet in private because I am afraid to have meetings in public. I bless the Lord that my heart is at that point, that if any man can lay anything to my charge, either in doctrine or practice, in this particular, that can be proved error or heresy, I am willing to disown it, even in the very market-place; but if it be truth, then to stand to it to the last drop of my blood. And, sir, said I, you ought to commend me for so doing. To err and to be a heretic are two things; I am no heretic, because I will not stand refractorily to defend any one thing that is contrary to the Word. Prove anything which I hold to be an error, and I will recant it.

COBB. But, goodman Bunyan, said he, methinks you need not stand so strictly upon this one thing, as to have meetings of such public assemblies. Cannot you submit, and, notwithstanding, do as much good as you can, in a neighbourly way, without having such meetings?

BUN. Truly, sir, said I, I do not desire to commend

myself, but to think meanly of myself; yet when I do most despise myself, taking notice of that small measure of light which God hath given me, also that the people of the Lord, by their own saying, are edified thereby. Besides, when I see that the Lord, through grace, hath in some measure blessed my labour, I dare not but exercise that gift which God hath given me for the good of the people. And I said further, that I would willingly speak in public, if I might.

COBB. He said, that I might come to the public assemblies and hear. What though you do not preach? you may hear. Do not think yourself so well enlightened, and that you have received a gift so far above others, but that you may hear other men preach. Or to that purpose.

BUN. I told him, I was as willing to be taught as to give instruction, and I looked upon it as my duty to do both; for, said I, a man that is a teacher, he himself may learn also from another that teacheth, as the apostle saith: "Ye may all prophesy, one by one, that all may learn" (*1 Cor. xiv. 31*). That is, every man that hath received a gift from God, he may dispense it, that others may be comforted; and when he hath done, he may hear and learn, and be comforted himself of others.

COBB. But, said he, what if you should forbear awhile, and sit still, till you see further how things will go?

BUN. Sir, said I, Wyclif saith, that he which leaveth off preaching and hearing of the Word of God for fear of excommunication of men, he is already excommunicated of God, and shall in the day of judgment be counted a traitor to Christ.

COBB. Aye, saith he, they that do not hear shall be so counted indeed; do you, therefore, hear.

BUN. But, sir, said I, he saith, he that shall leave off either preaching or hearing, etc. That is, if he hath received a gift of edification, it is his sin, if he doth not lay it out in a way of exhortation and counsel, according to the proportion of his gift; as well as to spend his time altogether in hearing others preach.

COBB. But, said he, how shall we know that you have received a gift?

BUN. Said I, Let any man hear and search, and prove the doctrine by the Bible.

COBB. But will you be willing, said he, that two indifferent persons shall determine the case, and will you stand by their judgment?

BUN. I said, Are they infallible?

COBB. He said, No.

BUN. Then, said I, it is possible my judgment may be as good as theirs. But yet I will pass by either, and in this matter be judged by the Scriptures; I am sure that is infallible, and cannot err.

COBB. But, said he, who shall be judge between you, for you take the Scriptures one way, and they another?

BUN. I said, The Scripture should, and that by comparing one scripture with another; for that will open itself, if it be rightly compared. As, for instance, if under the different apprehensions of the word Mediator, you would know that truth of it, the Scriptures open it, and tell us that he that is a mediator must take up the business between two, and "a mediator is not a mediator of one, but God is one," and "*there is* one mediator between God and men, even the man Christ Jesus" (*Gal. iii. 20; 1 Tim. ii. 5*). So likewise the Scripture calleth Christ a complete, or perfect, or able high priest. That is opened in that he is called man, and also God. His blood also is discovered to be effectually efficacious by the same things. So the Scripture, as touching the matter of meeting together, etc., doth likewise sufficiently open itself and discover its meaning.

COBB. But are you willing, said he, to stand to the judgment of the church?

BUN. Yes, sir, said I, to the approbation of the church of God; the church's judgment is best expressed in Scripture. We had much other discourse which I cannot well remember, about the laws of the nation, and submission to government; to which I did tell him, that I did look upon myself as bound in conscience to walk according to all righteous laws, and that whether there was a kind or no; and if I did anything that was contrary, I did hold it my duty to bear patiently the penalty of the

law, that was provided against such offenders; with
many more words to the like effect. And said, moreover,
that to cut off all occasions of suspicion from any, as
touching the harmlessness of my doctrine in private, I
would willingly take the pains to give anyone the notes of
all my sermons; for I do sincerely desire to live quietly in
my country, and to submit to the present authority.

COBB. Well, neighbour Bunyan, said he, but indeed I
would wish you seriously to consider of these things,
between this and the quarter-sessions, and to submit
yourself. You may do much good if you continue still in
the land; but alas, what benefit will it be to your friends,
or what good can you do to them, if you should be sent
away beyond the seas into Spain, or Constantinople, or
some other remote part of the world? Pray be ruled.

JAILER. Indeed, sir, I hope he will be ruled.

BUN. I shall desire, said I, in all godliness and honesty,
to behave myself in the nation, whilst I am in it. And if I
must be so dealt withal, as you say, I hope God will help
me to bear what they shall lay upon me. I know no evil
that I have done in this matter, to be so used. I speak as
in the presence of God.

COBB. You know, saith he, that the Scripture saith,
"the powers that be are ordained of God."

BUN. I said, Yes, and that I was to submit to the king
as supreme, also to the governors, as to them that are
sent by him.

COBB. Well then, said he, the king then commands you
that you should not have any private meetings; because
it is against his law, and he is ordained of God, therefore
you should not have any.

BUN. I told him that Paul did own the powers that were
in his day, as to be of God; and yet he was often in prison
under them for all that. And also, though Jesus Christ
told Pilate, that he had no power against him, but of
God, yet he died under the same Pilate; and yet, said I, I
hope you will not say that either Paul, or Christ, were
such as did deny magistracy, and so sinned against God
in slighting the ordinance. Sir, said I, the law hath
provided two ways of obeying: The one to do that which

I, in my conscience, do believe that I am bound to do, actively; and where I cannot obey actively, there I am willing to lie down, and to suffer what they shall do unto me. At this he sat still, and said no more; which, when he had done, I did thank him for his civil and meek discoursing with me; and so we parted

O that we might meet in heaven!

Farewell.   J B.

Here followeth a discourse between my Wife and the Judges, with others, touching my Deliverance at the Assizes following; the which I took from her own Mouth

After that I had received this sentence of banishing, or hanging, from them, and after the former admonition, touching the determination of the justices, if I did not recant; just when the time drew nigh, in which I should have abjured, or have done worse, as Mr. Cobb told me, came the time in which the king was to be crowned. Now, at the coronation of kings, there is usually a releasement of divers prisoners, by virtue of his coronation; in which privilege also I should have had my share; but that they took me for a convicted person, and therefore, unless I sued out a pardon, as they called it, I could have no benefit thereby; notwithstanding, yet, forasmuch as the coronation proclamation did give liberty, from the day the king was crowned to that day twelvemonth, to sue them out; therefore, though they would not let me out of prison, as they let out thousands, yet they could not meddle with me, as touching the execution of their sentence; because of the liberty offered for the suing out of pardons. Whereupon I continued in prison till the next assizes, which are called Midsummer assizes, being then kept in August 1661.

Now, at that assizes, because I would not leave any possible means unattempted that might be lawful, I did, by my wife, present a petition to the judges three times, that I might be heard, and that they would impartially take my case into consideration.

The first time my wife went, she presented it to Judge Hale, who very mildly received it at her hand, telling her that he would do her and me the best good he could; but he feared, he said, he could do none. The next day, again, lest they should, through the multitude of business, forget me, we did throw another petition into the coach to Judge Twisdon; who, when he had seen it, snapt her up, and angrily told her that I was a convicted person, and could not be released, unless I would promise to preach no more, etc.

Well, after this, she yet again presented another to Judge Hale, as he sat on the bench, who, as it seemed, was willing to give her audience. Only Justice Chester being present, stept up and said, that I was convicted in the court, and that I was a hot-spirited fellow, or words to that purpose, whereat he waived it, and did not meddle therewith. But yet, my wife being encouraged by the high sheriff, did venture once more into their presence, as the poor widow did to the unjust judge, to try what she could do with them for my liberty, before they went forth of the town. The place where she went to them was to the Swan Chamber, where the two judges, and many justices and gentry of the country, were in company together. She then, coming into the chamber with abashed face, and a trembling heart, began her errand to them in this manner:

WOMAN. My lord (directing herself to Judge Hale), I make bold to come once again to your lordship, to know what may be done with my husband.

JUDGE HALE. To whom he said, Woman, I told thee before, I could do thee no good; because they have taken that for a conviction which thy husband spoke at the sessions; and unless there be something done to undo that, I can do thee no good.

WOM. My lord, said she, he is kept unlawfully in prison; they clapped him up before there was any proclamation against the meetings; the indictment also is false. Besides, they never asked him whether he was guilty or no; neither did he confess the indictment.

ONE OF THE JUSTICES. Then one of the justices that

stood by, whom she knew not, said, My lord, he was lawfully convicted.

WOM. It is false, said she; for when they said to him, Do you confess the indictment? he said only this, that he had been at several meetings, both where there was preaching the Word, and prayer, and that they had God's presence among them.

JUDGE TWISDON. Whereat Judge Twisdon answered very angrily, saying, What! you think we can do what we list; your husband is a breaker of the peace, and is convicted by the law, etc. Whereupon Judge Hale called for the Statute Book.

WOM. But, said she, my lord, he was not lawfully convicted.

CHESTER. Then Justice Chester said, My lord, he was lawfully convicted.

WOM. It is false, said she; it was but a word of discourse that they took for a conviction, as you heard before.

CHEST. But it is recorded, woman, it is recorded, said Juctice Chester; as if it must be of necessity true, because it was recorded. With which words he often endeavoured to stop her mouth, having no other argument to convince her, but "it is recorded, it is recorded."

WOM. My lord, said she, I was a while since at London, to see if I could get my husband's liberty; and there I spoke with my Lord Barkwood, one of the House of Lords, to whom I delivered a petition, who took it of me and presented it to some of the rest of the House of Lords, for my husband's releasement; who, when they had seen it, they said that they could not release him, but had committed his releasement to the judges, at the next assizes. This he told me; and now I come to you to see if anything may be done in this business, and you give neither releasement nor belief. To which they gave her no answer, but made as if they heard her not.

CHEST. Only Justice Chester was often up with this, "He is convicted," and "It is recorded."

WOM. If it be, it is false, said she.

CHEST. My lord, said Justice Chester, he is a pestilent fellow, there is not such a fellow in the country again.

TWIS. What, will your husband leave preaching? If he will do so, then send for him.

WOM. My lord, said she, he dares not leave preaching, as long as he can speak.

TWIS. See here, what should we talk any more about such a fellow? Must he do what he lists? He is a breaker of the peace.

WOM. She told him again, that he desired to live peaceably, and to follow his calling, that his family might be maintained; and, moreover, said, My lord, I have four small children that cannot help themselves, of which one is blind, and have nothing to live upon, but the charity of good people.

HALE. Hast thou four children? said Judge Hale; thou art but a young woman to have four children.

WOM. My lord, said she, I am but mother-in-law to them, having not been married to him yet full two years. Indeed, I was with child when my husband was first apprehended; but being young, and unaccustomed to such things, said she, I being smayed at the news, fell into labour, and so continued for eight days, and then was delivered, but my child died.

HALE. Whereat, he looking very soberly on the matter, said, Alas, poor woman!

TWIS. But Judge Twisdon told her, that she made poverty her cloak; and said, moreover, that he understood I was maintained better by running up and down a-preaching, than by following my calling.

HALE. What is his calling? said Judge Hale.

ANSWER. Then some of the company that stood by said, A tinker, my lord.

WOM. Yes, said she, and because he is a tinker, and a poor man, therefore he is despised, and cannot have justice.

HALE. Then Judge Hale answered, very mildly, saying, I tell thee, woman, seeing it is so, that they have taken what thy husband spake for a conviction; thou must either apply thyself to the king, or sue out his pardon, or get a writ of error.

CHEST. But when Justice Chester heard him give her

this counsel; and especially, as she supposed, because he spoke of a writ of error, he chafed, and seemed to be very much offended; saying, My lord he will preach and do what he lists.

WOM. He preacheth nothing but the Word of God, said she.

TWIS. He preach the Word of God! said Twisdon; and withal she thought he would have struck her; he runneth up and down, and doth harm.

WOM. No, my lord, said she, it is not so; God hath owned him, and done much good by him.

TWIS. God! said he; his doctrine is the doctrine of the devil.

WOM. My lord, she said, when the righteous Judge shall appear, it will be known that his doctrine is not the doctrine of the devil.

TWIS. My lord, said he, to Judge Hale, do not mind her, but send her away.

HALE. Then said Judge Hale, I am sorry, woman, that I can do thee no good; thou must do one of those three things aforesaid; namely, either to apply thyself to the king, or sue out his pardon, or get a writ of error; but a writ of error will be cheapest.

WOM. At which Chester again seemed to be in a chafe, and put off his hat, and as she thought, scratched his head for anger: but when I saw, said she, that there was no prevailing to have my husband sent for, though I often desired them that they would send for him, that he might speak for himself, telling them, that he could give them better satisfaction than I could in what they demanded of him, with several other things, which now I forget; only this I remember, that though I was somewhat timorous at my first entrance into the chamber, yet before I went out, I could not but break forth into tears, not so much because they were so hard-hearted against me and my husband, but to think what a sad account such poor creatures will have to give at the coming of the Lord, when they shall there answer for all things whatsoever they have done in the body, whether it be good or whether it be bad.

So, when I departed from them, the Book of Statute was brought, but what they said of it I know nothing at all, neither did I hear any more from them.

Some Carriages of the Adversaries of God's Truth with me at the next Assizes, which was on the 19th of the First Month, 1662

I shall pass by what befal between these two assizes, how I had, by my jailer, some liberty granted me, more than at the first, and how I followed my wonted course of preaching, taking all occasions that were put into my hand to visit the people of God; exhorting them to be steadfast in the faith of Jesus Christ, and to take heed that they touched not the Common Prayer, etc., but to mind the Word of God, which giveth direction to Christians in every point, being able to make the man of God perfect in all things through faith in Jesus Christ, and thoroughly to furnish him unto all good works (*2 Tim. iii. 17*). Also, how I, having, I say, somewhat more liberty, did go to see Christians at London; which my enemies hearing of, were so angry, that they had almost cast my jailer out of his place, threatening to indict him, and to do what they could against him. They charged me also, that I went thither to plot and raise division, and make insurrection, which, God knows, was a slander; whereupon my liberty was more straitened than it was before: so that I must not look out of the door. Well, when the next sessions came, which was about the 10th of the eleventh month, I did expect to have been very roundly dealt withal; but they passed me by, and would not call me, so that I rested till the assizes, which was the 19th of the first month following; and when they came, because I had a desire to come before the judge, I desired my jailer to put my name into the calendar among the felons, and made friends of the judge and high sheriff, who promised that I should be called; so that I thought what I had done might have beem effectual for the obtaining of my desire; but all was in vain: for when the assizes came, though my name was in the calendar, and also though both the judge and sheriff had promised that I should appear before them, yet the justices and the clerk of the peace did so work it about, that I, notwithstanding, was deferred, and might not appear; and although, I say, I do not know of all their carriages towards me, yet this I know, that the clerk of the peace did discover himself to be one of my greatest opposers: for, first, he came to my jailer, and told him that I must not go down before the judge, and therefore must not be put into the calendar; to whom my jailer said, that my name was in already. He bid him put me out again; my jailer told him that he could not, for he had given the judge a calendar with my name in it, and also the sheriff another. At which he was very much displeased, and desired to see that calendar that was yet in my jailer's hand; who, when he had given it him, he looked on it, and said it was a false calendar; he also took the calendar and blotted out my accusation, as my jailer had writ it. Which accusation I cannot tell what it was, because it was so blotted out; and he himself put in words to this purpose: "That John Bunyan was committed to prison, being lawfully convicted for upholding of unlawful meetings and conventicles," etc. But yet, for all this, fearing that what he had done, unless he added thereto, it would not do; he first run to the clerk of the assizes, then to the justices, and afterwards, because he would not leave any means unattempted to hinder me, he comes again to my jailer, and tells him, that if I did go down before the judge, and was released, he would make him pay my fees, which, he said, was due to him; and further told him, that he would complain of him at the next quarter-sessions for making of false calendars; though my jailer himself, as I afterwards learned, had put in my accusation worse than in itself it was by far. And thus was I hindered and prevented, at that time also, from appearing before the judge, and left in prison.

Farewell.

JOHN BUNYAN.

A CONTINUATION OF MR. BUNYAN'S LIFE; BEGINNING WHERE HE LEFT OFF, AND CONCLUDING WITH THE TIME AND MANNER OF HIS DEATH AND BURIAL, TOGETHER WITH HIS TRUE CHARACTER

Reader, the painful and industrious author of this book has already given you a faithful and very moving relation of the beginning and middle of the days of his pilgrimage on earth; and since there yet remains somewhat worthy of notice and regard, which occurred in the last scence of his life; the which, for want of time, or fear that some over-censorious people should impute it to him, as an earnest coverting of praise from men, he has not left behind him in writing. Wherefore, as a true friend and long acquaintance of Mr. Bunyan's that his good end may be known as well as his evil beginning, I have taken upon me, from my knowledge, and the best account given by other of his friends, to piece this to the thread, too soon broke off, and so lengthen it out to his entering upon eternity.

He has told you at large of his birth and education; the evil habits and corruptions of his youth; the temptations he struggled and conflicted so frequently with; the mercies, comforts, and deliverances he found; how he came to take upon him the preaching of the gospel; the slanders, reproaches, and imprisonments that attended him; and the progress he notwithstanding made, by the assistance of God's grace, no doubt to the saving of many souls. Therefore take these things as he himself has methodically laid them down in the words of verity; and so I pass on as to what remains.

After his being freed from his twelve years' imprisonment and upwards, for nonconformity, wherein he had time to furnish the world with sundry good books, etc.; and, by his patience, to move Dr. Barlow, the then Bishop of Lincoln, and other churchmen, to pity his hard and unreasonable sufferings, so far as to stand very much his friends in procuring his enlargement, or there perhaps he had died by the noisomeness and ill usage of the place; being now, I say, again at liberty, and having, through mercy, shaken off his bodily fetters, for those upon his soul were broken before, by the abounding grace that filled his heart, he went to visit those that had been a comfort to him in his tribulation, with a Christian-like acknowledgment of their kindness and enlargement of charity; giving encouragement by his example if it happened to be their hard haps to fall into affliction or trouble, then to suffer patiently for the sake of a good conscience, and for the love of God in Jesus Christ towards their souls; and, by many cordial persuasions, supported some whose spirits began to sink low through the fear of danger that threatened their worldly concernment, so that the people found a wonderful consolation in his discourse and admonitions.

As often as opportunity would admit, he gathered them together in convenient places, though the law was then in force against meetings, and fed them with the sincere milk of the Word, that they might grow up in grace thereby. To such as were anywhere taken and imprisoned upon these accounts, he made it another part of his business to extend his charity, and gather relief for such of them as wanted.

He took great care to visit the sick, and strengthen them against the suggestions of the tempter, which at such times are very prevalent; so that they had cause for ever to bless God, who had put into his heart, at such a time, to rescue them from the power of the roaring lion, who sought to devour them; nor did he spare any pains or labour in travel, though to the remote counties, where he knew, or imagined, any people might stand in need of his assistance, insomuch that some of these visitations that he made, which was two or three every year, some, though in jeering manner, no doubt, gave him the epithet of Bishop Bunyan, whilst others envied him for his so earnestly labouring in Christ's vineyard, yet the seed of the World he, all this while, sowed in the hearts of his congregation, watered with the grace of God, brought forth in abundance, in bringing in disciples to the church of Christ.

Another part of his time he spent in reconciling differences, by which he hindered many mischiefs, and saved some families from ruin; and, in such fallings out, he was uneasy, till he found a means to labour a reconciliation, and become a peacemaker, on whom a blessing is promised in Holy Writ; and, indeed, in doing this good office, he may be said to sum up his days, it being the last undertaking of his life, as will appear in the close of his paper.

When, in the late reign, liberty of conscience was unexpectedly given and indulged to Dissenters of all persuasions, his piercing wit penetrated the veil, and found that it was not for the Dissenters' sake they were so suddenly freed from the prosecutions that had long lain heavy upon them, and set, in a manner, on an equal foot with the Church of England, which the Papists were undermining, and about to subvert. He foresaw all the advantages that could have redounded to the Dissenters, would have been no more than what Poliphemus, the monstrous giant of Sicily, would have allowed Ulysses, viz. That he would eat his men first, and do him the favour of being eaten last. For, although Mr. Bunyan, following the examples of others, did lay hold of this liberty, as an acceptable thing in itself, knowing that God is the only lord of conscience, and that it is good at all times to do according to the dictates of a good conscience, and that the preaching the glad tidings of the gospel is beautiful in the preacher; yet, in all this, he moved with caution and a holy fear, earnestly praying for averting the impendent judgments, which he saw like a black tempest hanging over our heads, for our sins, and ready to break upon us, and that the Ninevites' remedy was now highly necessary. Hereupon, he gathered his congregation at Bedford, where he mostly lived, and had lived, and had spent the greatest part of his life; and there being no convenient place to be had, for the entertainment of so great a confluence of people as followed him, upon the account of his teaching, he consulted with them for the building of a meeting house; to which they made their voluntary contributions, with all cheerfulness and alacrity; and the first time he appeared there to edify, the place was so thronged, that many were constrained to stay without, though the house was very spacious, everyone striving to partake of his instructions, that were of his persuasion; and show their good will towards him, by being present at the opening of the place; and here he lived in much peace and quiet of mind, contenting himself with that little God has bestowed upon him, and sequestering himself from all secular employments to follow that of his call to the ministry; for, as God said to Moses, he that made the lips and heart, can give eloquence and wisdom, without extraordinary acquirements in a university.

During these things, there were regulators sent into all cities and towns corporate, to new-model the government in the magistracy, etc., by turning out some, and putting in others. Against this, Mr. Bunyan expressed his zeal with some weariness, as foreseeing the bad consequences that would attend it, and laboured with his congregation to prevent their being imposed on in this kind; and when a great man in those days, coming to Bedford upon some such errand, sent for him, as it is supposed, to give him a place of public trust, he would by no means come at him, but sent his excuse.

When he was at leisure from writing and teaching, he often came up to London, and there went among the congregations of the nonconformists, and used his talent to the great good liking of the hearers; and even some, to whom he had been misrepresented, upon the account of his education, were convinced of his worth and knowledge in sacred things, as perceiving him to be a man of sound judgment, delivering himself plainly and powerfully; insomuch that many who came as mere spectators, for novelty's sake, rather than to be edified and improved, went away well satisfied with what they heard, and wondered, as the Jews did at the apostles, viz. whence this man should have these things; perhaps not considering that God more immediately assists those that make it their business industriously and cheerfully to labour in his vineyard.

Thus he spent his latter years, in imitation of his great Lord and Master, the ever-blessed Jesus; he went about doing good, so that the most prying critic, or even malice herself, is defied to find, even upon the narrowest search or observation, any sully or stain upon his reputation with which he may be justly charged; and this we note as a challenge to those that have had the least regard for him, or them of his persuasion, and have, one way or other, appeared in the front of those that oppressed him, and for the turning whose hearts, in obedience to the commission and commandment given him of God, he frequently prayed, and sometimes sought a blessing for them, even with tears, the effects of which they may, peradventure, though undeservedly, have found in their persons, friends, relations, or estates; for God will hear the prayers of the faithful, and answer them, even for those that vex them, as it happened in the case of Job's praying for the three persons that had been grievous in their reproach against him, even in the day of his sorrow.

But yet let me come a little nearer to particulars and periods of time for the better refreshing the memories of those that knew his labour and suffering, and for the satisfaction of all that shall read this book.

After he was sensibly convicted of the wicked state of his life, and converted, he was baptised into the congregation and admitted a member thereof, viz. in the year 1655, and became speedily a very zealous professor; but, upon the return of King Charles to the crown, in 1660, he was, on the 12th of November, taken, as he was edifying some good people that were got together to hear the Word, and confined in Bedford jail for the space of six years, till the Act of Indulgence to Dissenters being allowed, he obtained his freedom by the intercession of some in trust and power that took pity of his sufferings; but within six years afterwards [from his first imprisonment] he was again taken up, viz. in the year 1666, and was then confined for six years more, when even the jailer took such pity of his rigorous sufferings that he did as the Egyptian jailer did to Joseph, put all the care and trust into his hands. When he was taken this last time, he was preaching on these words, viz. "Dost thou believe on the Son of God?" and this imprisonment continued six years; and when this was over, another short affliction, which was an imprisonment of half a year, fell to his share. During these confinements he wrote these following books, viz.: *Of Prayer by the Spirit, The Holy City, Resurrection, Grace Abounding, Pilgrim's Progress,* the first part.

In the last year of his twelve years' imprisonment, the pastor of the congregation of Bedford died, and he was chosen to that care of souls on the 12th of December, 1671. And in this his charge he often had disputes with scholars, that came to oppose him, as supposing him an ignorant person, and thought he argued plainly and by Scripture without phrases and logical expressions; yet he nonplussed one who came to oppose him in his congregation, by demanding whether or no we had the true copies of the original Scriptures; and another, when he was preaching, accused him of uncharitableness, for saying. It was very hard for most to be saved; saying, by that, he went about to exclude most of his congregation; but he confuted him and put him to silence with the parable of the stony ground and other texts out of the 13th of Matthew, in our Saviour's sermon out of a ship, all his method being to keep close to the Scriptures; and what he found not warranted there, himself would not warrant nor determine, unless in such cases as were plain, wherein no doubts or scruples did arise.

But not to make any further mention of this kind, it is well known that this person managed all his affairs with such exactness as if he had made it his study, above all other things, not to give occasion of offence, but rather suffer many inconveniencies to avoid; being never heard to reproach or revile any, what injury soever he received, but rather to rebuke those that did; and as it was in his conversation, so it is manifested in those books he has caused to be published to the world; where, like the archangel disputing with Satan about the body of Moses, as we find it in the epistle of Jude, he brings no railing accusation, but leaves the rebukers, those that persecuted him, to the Lord.

In his family he kept up a very strict discipline in prayer and exhortations; being in this like Joshua, as that good man expresses it, viz. Whatsoever others did, as for me and my house, we will serve the Lord; and, indeed, a blessing waited on his labours and endeavours, so that his wife, as the Psalmist says, was like a pleasant vine upon the walls of his house, and his children like olive branches round his table; for so shall it be with the man that fears the Lord; and though by reason of the many losses he sustained by imprisonment and spoil, of his chargeable sickness, etc., his earthly treasures swelled not to excess, he always had sufficient to live decently and creditably, and with that he had the greatest of all treasures, which is content; for, as the wise man says, that is a continual feast.

But where content dwells, even a poor cottage is a kingly palace; and this happiness he had all his life long, not so much minding this world as knowing he was here as a pilgrim and stranger, and had no tarrying city, but looking for one not made with hands, eternal in the highest heavens; but at length, worn out with sufferings, age, and often teaching, the day of his dissolution drew near, and death, that unlocks the prison of the soul, to enlarge it for a more glorious mansion, put a stop to his acting his part on the stage of mortality; heaven, like earthly princes when it threatens war, being always so kind as to call home its ambassadors before it be denounced; and even the last act or undertaking of his was a labour of love and charity; for it so falling out, that a young gentleman, a neighbour of Mr. Bunyan, happening into the displeasure of his father, and being much troubled in mind upon that account, as also for that he had heard his father purposed to disinherit him, or otherwise deprive him of what he had to leave, he pitched upon Mr. Bunyan as a fit man to make way for his submission, and prepare his father's mind to receive him; and he, as willing to do any good office as it could be requested, as readily undertook it; and so, riding to Reading, in Berkshire, he then there used such pressing arguments and reasons against anger and passion, as also for love and reconciliation, that the father was mollified, and his bowels yearned towards his returning son.

But Mr. Bunyan, after he had disposed all things to the best for accommodation, returning to London, and being overtaken with excessive rains, coming to his lodging extreme wet, fell sick of a violent fever, which he bore with much constancy and patience; and expressed himself as if he desired nothing more than to be dissolved, and to be with Christ, in the case esteeming death as gain, and life only a tedious delaying of felicity expected; and finding his vital strength decay, having settled his mind and affairs, as well as the shortness of his time and the violence of his disease would admit, with a constant and Christian patience, he resigned his soul into the hands of his most merciful Redeemer, following his pilgrim from the City of Destruction to the New Jerusalem; his better part having been all along there, in holy contemplation, pantings, and breathings after the hidden manna, and water of life; as by many holy and humble consolations expressed in his letters to several persons, in prison and out of prison, too many to be here inserted at present. He died at the house of one Mr. Straddocks, a grocer, at the Star on Snowhill, in the parish of St. Sepulchre, London, on the 12th of August, 1688, and in the sixtieth year of his age, after ten days' sickness; and was buried in the new burying place near the Artillery Ground; where he sleeps to the morning of the resurrection, in hopes of a glorious rising to an incorruptible immortality of joy and happiness; where no more trouble and sorrow shall afflict him, but all tears be wiped away; when the just shall be incorrupted, as members of Christ their head, and reign with him as kings and priests for ever.

A BRIEF CHARACTER OF MR. JOHN BUNYAN

He appeared in countenance to be of a stern and rough temper; but in his conversation mild and affable, not given to loquacity or much discourse in company, unless some urgent occasion required it; observing never to boast of himself, or his parts, but rather seem low in his own eyes, and submit himself to the judgment of others; abhorring lying and swearing, being just in all that lay in his power to his word, not seeming to revenge injuries, loving to reconcile differences, and make friendship with all; he had a sharp quick eye, accomplished with an excellent discerning of persons, being of good judgment and quick wit. As for his person, he was tall of statute, strong-boned, though not corpulent, somewhat of a ruddy face, with sparkling eyes, wearing his hair on his upper lip, after the old British fashion; his hair reddish, but in his latter days, time had sprinkled it with grey; his nose well set, but not declining or bending, and his mouth moderate large; his forehead something high, and his habit always plain and modest. And thus have we impartially described the internal and external parts of a person, whose death hath been much regretted; a person who had tried the smiles and frowns of time; not puffed up in prosperity, nor shaken in adversity, always holding the golden mean.

> "In him at once did three great worthies shine,
> Historian, poet, and a choice divine;
> Then let him rest in undisturbèd dust,
> Until the resurrection of the just."

POSTSCRIPT

In this his pilgrimage, God blessed him with four children, one of which, named Mary, was blind, and died some years before; his other children are Thomas, Joseph, and Sarah; and his wife Elizabeth, having lived to see him overcome his labour and sorrow, and pass from this life to receive the reward of his works, long survived him not, but in 1692 she died; to follow her faithful pilgrim from this world to the other, whither he was gone before her; while his works, which consist of sixty books, remain for the edifying of the reader, and the praise of the author.—*Vale.*